Communicating Doors

Born in London in 1939, Alan Ayckbourn spent most of his childhood in Sussex and was educated at Haileybury. Leaving there one Friday at the age of seventeen, he went into the theatre the following Monday and has been working at it ever since as, variously, a stage manager, sound technician, lighting technician, scene painter, prop-maker, actor, writer and director. These talents developed thanks to his mentor, Stephen Joseph, whom he first met in 1958 upon joining the newly formed Library Theatre in Scarborough. He was a BBC Radio drama producer from 1965 to 1970, returning to Scarborough to take up the post of artistic director of the Theatre in the Round, left vacant after Stephen Joseph's death in 1967. He has premièred over forty of his plays at this Yorkshire theatre where he spends the greater part of the year directing other people's work. Some twenty-nine of his plays have subsequently been produced either in the West End, at the RNT or the RSC. They have been translated into forty languages and have been performed throughout the world, receiving many national and international awards in the process.

by the same author

ALAN AYCKBOURN

Communicating Doors

faber and faber
LONDON · BOSTON

First published in 1995
by Faber and Faber Limited
3 Queen Square London WC1N 3AU

Photoset by Parker Typesetting Service, Leicester
Printed in England by Mackays of Chatham PLC

A CIP record for this book
is available from the British Library

ISBN 0–571–17682–8

2 4 6 8 10 9 7 5 3

Characters

Reece, a businessman aged 30 and 70
Jessica, his first wife aged 25 and 45
Ruella, his second wife aged 45
Julian, his business associate aged 45 and 65
Phoebe (Poopay), a prostitute aged 33
Harold, a house detective aged 35 and 55

A suite in the Regal Hotel, London WC2

Time
May 1974
October 1994
July 2014

Communicating Doors was first performed in
Scarborough at the Stephen Joseph Theatre in the Round,
on 2 February 1994. The cast was as follows:

Reece John Hudson
Jessica Sara Markland
Ruella Liz Crowther
Julian Richard Durden
Poopay Adie Allen
Harold Nick Stringer

Director Alan Ayckbourn
Designer Roger Glossop
Lighting Mick Hughes
Music John Pattison

It was first performed in London in August 1995.
The cast was as follows:

Reece Laurence Kennedy
Jessica Sara Markland
Ruella Julia McKenzie
Julian Ken Bones
Poopay Adie Allen
Harold John Arthur

Director Alan Ayckbourn
Designer Roger Glossop
Lighting Mick Hughes
Music John Pattison

Act One

It is the year 2014. A view of part of a sixth-floor suite in the five-star Regal Hotel. Our view is of the sitting room and the bathroom. At least four doors lead off the sitting room: the main door leading straight on to the hallway; one linking direct to the bathroom; one leading to the bedroom; the fourth is an intercommunicating door to the room next door. This last door will play a significant part in the action. It opens inwards permitting one person – just – to squeeze into a small cupboard-like space or lobby (also visible). Once the occupant has closed this door behind them, only then is there space to open the further door, i.e. both doors cannot be opened simultaneously. Moreover, this entire two-door/lobby unit should be built to revolve so that either door can open on to the area in view.

The bathroom has two doors; the one previously mentioned, leading to the sitting room; a second leading to the bedroom.

This suite itself will need to alter very swiftly as the action proceeds in order to reflect various locations (and time periods). This can be done primarily with light and a certain scenic ingenuity.

The rooms, basically, have a fairly classic architectural feel with high, imposing Victorian ceilings and solid classic furniture. The sitting room has a long sofa, an armchair, a writing desk and chair, a sideboard that incorporates the mini-bar, plus other furnishings including a small phone table. It also has some rather splendid high windows that open on to a shallow, high-level balcony. Six floors below this is the street; across the street is the river. The window

*curtains are, in the main, left open. The bathroom
contains all the usual fittings: a bath/shower, WC, bidet,
bathroom cabinet, towel rails, etc.*

At the start it is summer evening in July, around 9 p.m.

Julian, *a tall, powerful man, stands staring out of the
windows. The sound of distant small arms fire and the
occasional mortar explosion can be heard, momentarily,
from across the river. Now aged sixty-five, he is still in
good physical shape. He is very well spoken in a way that
suggests that his original background could have been
vastly different. Despite the time of year, he is smartly
dressed in an expensive dark suit. After a second or so, the
doorbell chimes. Julian turns and goes to answer the door.
As he does so, he calls to someone, unseen, in the
bedroom.*

Julian (*as he goes, calling*) She's here.

> *There is no reply from the bedroom. Julian opens the
> door to admit* **Poopay.** *She is blonde, heavily made-up,
> aged thirty plus but having a fair stab at twenty-five
> minus. She is swathed in a long, almost ankle length,
> high-collared, artificial fur coat and carries an
> incongruously large leather bag filled with the tools of
> her trade. She is unmistakably a class, but not that high
> class, hooker.*

Poopay (*sweetly*) Hallo. I'm Poopay.

Julian (*startled*) What?

Poopay Poopay. Lennox sent me. I understand you –
Have I the right room?

> *Julian nods her into the room and closes the door
> behind her. As he does this, he looks her up and down
> with ill-concealed contempt. Poopay is unaware of this.
> She looks around.*

2

Oh, this is nice. Very nice. Got the suite, have you? Yes. Beautiful. (*She now goes straight into her stern nanny/ schoolmistress act.*) Now, what's this I've been hearing? You've been a very naughty boy, haven't you? So I've been told. Don't try and deny it. You've been very, very bad, haven't you? Well. We'll soon see about that, won't we? We'll soon put a stop to that. Just wait and see what Poopay's got for you in here, my lad.

> *She puts her bag down with a clank. During the next she starts to unfasten her coat. She talks as from a well- worn script, staring out of the windows as she talks, her mind on a dozen other things. Julian, meantime, has moved to the bedroom door.*

She's going to teach you a lesson you won't forget in a hurry, I can promise you. A little punishment, a little strict discipline, that's what you're in need of, aren't you? Well, just you wait. By the time I've finished with you, my boy, you'll learn to control yourself. (*She has taken off her coat to reveal her full 'dominatrix' outfit'.*) Now, I want you to go straight in that bedroom and take off all your . . . (*She breaks off as she sees that Julian isn't paying attention.*)

Julian (*calling through the bedroom doorway again*) She's arrived . . .

Reece (*off, from the bedroom*) What?

Julian (*calling*) She's here. The tart's here.

Reece (*off*) All right. Just a minute. Tell her to wait a minute, Julian.

Poopay (*dropping her previous tone*) Excuse me. Am I to understand there are two of you?

Julian What?

Poopay Because Lennox lead me to believe there was just

3

one gentleman here requiring my services . . . That this was a single engagement . . .

Julian There's only one.

Poopay Only if this turns out to be a group booking, then the rates are very different –

Julian Just the one.

Poopay I mean, don't get me wrong, I'm happy to accommodate two but I think you should be warned that I –

Julian (*more sharply*) Just the one, all right?

Poopay (*slightly warily*) Right. (*suspiciously*) Where are you going to be, then? Only if you intend watching, it still counts as –

Julian (*cutting her off*) I shall be elsewhere.

Reece (*off*) Tell her I'm just coming, Julian.

Julian (*to Poopay*) I asked for Delphine. Where's Delphine?

Poopay Delphine? She's – off sick.

Julian Sick?

Poopay She – went down with something.

Julian I wanted Delphine.

Poopay Well, you've got me instead, haven't you? Anyway, it's not for you, is it? You've said.

Reece (*off*) Tell her I won't be long. (*He sounds as if he's struggling with something.*) Is she beautiful, then?

    Julian doesn't reply.

Poopay (*calling*) She's gorgeous.

Reece (*off, struggling*) Ah! She sounds a beauty. She sounds a lovely.

Poopay (*to Julian*) What's he doing in there?

Julian He's getting dressed.

Poopay (*mystified*) What's he getting dressed for?

Julian You know who you remind me of?

Poopay Who?

Julian My mother.

Poopay I'm sure we're both flattered.

Reece (*off, struggling*) I may – need – help – arrgh! – with these shoe laces again, Julian . . .

Julian (*calling but not moving*) Say the word, Reece.

Reece (*off*) Bloody things . . .

Poopay How old is he, then?

Julian Never mind.

Poopay I mean, if he can't even do his shoes up. I mean.

Julian (*with sudden urgency*) Listen, he's not in good health, so go carefully with him, all right. (*Indicating her bag.*) None of your fancy games or you'll finish him off. Just one quick straight screw and piss off.

Poopay (*starting to protest*) Listen, there is no need to talk to me like – (*She starts to put on her coat again.*)

Julian (*talking through her*) You keep all that stuff strictly in your bag.

Poopay – I'm not staying here to be –

Julian (*still ignoring her*) Look. (*He moves to the phone table.*) I will be in my room just along the corridor. I am writing the number here. If there is any problem, you contact me and only me –

Poopay I'm sorry, I am not –

Julian Understood?

Poopay – not being responsible for someone who's not fully –

Julian (*quietly*) Hey! Hey! Are you listening to me?

A slight pause. Poopay weighs him up as someone not to argue with.

Poopay Yes. (*more warily*) All I'm saying is, if the man . . . if the man is . . . then . . . maybe I shouldn't . . . he shouldn't . . . that's all I'm saying . . . that's all. (*Pause.*) I mean, come on. Be fair. Eh?

Reece enters. After the build up, he really isn't as old as all that – a mere seventy. Not a robust septuagenarian, though, but frail and apparently one with not too long to live. He moves with some difficulty and whenever he does, needs to pause frequently for breath. Once a handsome young man, a life of aggression, double dealing and ultimate disillusionment and disappointment have resulted in a testy individual, self-willed, old before his time, living a life of constant pain.

Reece Aha! Aha!

Poopay looks at him in horror.

So this is the – this is the – this is Lennox's young friend. He's got hidden depths, hasn't he? Our hall porter? Never get you a bloody taxi, but he can fix you up with a woman at the drop of his cocked hat. Come on then, get your coat off, girl. Julian, take her coat for her. You haven't even taken the woman's coat.

Poopay That's all right.

Julian Give me your coat.

Reece Take her coat, man –

Poopay No, I'll keep it on, thank you.

Julian (*sharply*) You heard him, give me your coat.

Poopay looks from one to the other and decides, reluctantly, to surrender her coat.

Reece That's better. (*to Poopay*) Very nice.

Poopay Thank you.

Reece Can't do – what we're going to be doing – with your coat on, can you? (*to Julian*) Hang it up for her, Julian, in my wardrobe. Then you can go.

Julian goes into the bedroom for a second.

Me and this young lady have – er – things to do in private. (*smiling at her*) Don't we?

Poopay (*doubtful*) Possibly.

Reece (*sitting on the sofa*) Sit down, sit down, then.

Poopay Right. (*She sits in the chair.*) I'm sorry I'm late. I think there was a gun battle in the Strand.

Reece Come on, a bit closer than that. I'm paying for this.

Poopay (*sitting next to him*) There were armoured cars everywhere . . .

Reece That's better.

Poopay Ever since that Houses of Parliament business . . .

Reece There.

He puts an arm round her shoulder. She doesn't respond.

Poopay Funny without Big Ben. Listen, I don't think this is going to –

Julian returns. He looks at them.

Julian All right?

Reece Very cosy. (*to Poopay*) Isn't it?

Poopay Wonderful. He's extremely sexy.

Reece Now be a good fellow and go away.

Julian Call me when you've done.

Reece I will.

Julian opens the front door.

I wouldn't wait up, though. (*He laughs.*)

Julian goes out, closing the door.

Poopay Listen, I'm sorry to disappoint you but I don't think this is going to work out at all . . .

Reece removes his arm from around her shoulder and starts to struggle to his feet.

You see, I'm a specialist – and my particular line is probably . . .

Reece Wait here! (*He starts to head towards the bathroom.*)

Poopay My particular speciality, well, it's – it's not designed – Where are you going?

Reece Wait! Wait! (*He goes into the bathroom, switching on the light.*)

Poopay (*following him*) You see, it's not really suitable for

8

maturer people. It's quite, you know, arduous – I mean not violent, you understand – I'm not into violence – just a bit of fun and pain, really . . . What the hell are you doing?

Reece is at the bidet, attempting to kneel down.

Reece (*struggling vainly*) Oh, this damned – ah! Can you do it? Can you reach it?

Poopay What?

Reece Down the waste pipe. Take out the plug and feel down the waste pipe.

Poopay I'm not putting my hand in there . . .

Reece Come on! It's perfectly clean. Come on. Just feel down with your fingers.

Poopay does as she's told, with some distaste.

Poopay I don't know what we're into here. You're *really* weird, you are.

Reece Can you feel it . . . ?

Poopay No, nothing. Just – Oh. Piece of paper. Is that it?

Reece That's it! Get it out.

Poopay retrieves three or four sheets of folded foolscap paper.

Poopay I dread to think what this is. Is this what you want?

Reece Give it here.

Poopay What do you keep it there for?

Reece Because it's the safest place I could think of.

Reece returns to the sitting room, switching off the bathroom light as he goes. Poopay follows.

Poopay Get wet there, won't it?

Reece Wet? Who the hell ever uses those things?

Poopay Why do you need to hide it in the first place?

Reece Because they're watching me all the time, that's why.

Poopay Are they? Who are?

Reece reaches the desk and starts to unfold the paper.

Reece Goodman. Any of them. Right, now. Let's get down to it. Pay attention.

Poopay Listen . . .

Reece No, you listen. Just shut your trap for a minute . . .

Poopay Listen, I cannot do this. I cannot go through with this, I'm sorry. That's all I'm saying. It's too risky. It's too dangerous. I had no idea of your – physical condition when I came up here. That bloody Lennox, he just books us in –

Reece What are you talking about?

Poopay I'm saying we can't do it. Right? Not possible to do. OK.

Reece Do what?

Poopay Sex.

Reece (*mystified*) Sex?

Poopay Yes. Sex. Remember it? Sex.

Reece Who the hell's talking about sex. I don't want sex.

Poopay You don't?

Reece Don't be stupid. Look at me, woman. Finish me off altogether, in my condition. Now sit down, pay attention and shut up. We haven't got much time.

Poopay (*sitting*) I don't know what's happening. I do not know what's occurring here.

Reece All I require from you, young woman, is one signature.

Poopay A what?

Reece A signature. Can you write your name? I presume you can write your name? Then that's all I want you to do. That and – to run a small errand.

Poopay Look, what is all this?

Reece Just sign your name here, come on. I'll pay you everything you want. Straight cash and away you go. Easiest money you'll ever earn in your life. Come on. Over here. Sign your name.

Poopay I'm not signing. Sorry.

Reece Why the hell not?

Poopay I don't even know what it is I'm signing.

Reece What does it matter? All you're doing is witnessing my signature, that's all. My signature to a document.

Poopay What sort of document? A will?

Reece Of course not a will. If it was a will, I'd get my lawyer in, have it done properly.

Poopay Why can't you get that one done properly?

Reece Because – (*impatiently*) What does it matter to you? Come on, are you going to sign or aren't you?

Poopay No. And don't shout at me. I don't like it.

Reece (*calmer*) You don't want your money, then?

Poopay I'll do without it, thank you very much.

Reece All right. I'll pay you double.

Poopay Sorry. No.

Reece Oh, my God. An honest whore. That's all I need . . .

Poopay No, not honest. Just not an idiot, that's all. And not a whore either, if you don't mind. I resent that term deeply.

Reece What else are you then?

Poopay I'm a Specialist Sexual Consultant.

Reece Oh, hooray! (*suddenly deflated*) So you refuse to sign? You won't do it? Then goodnight.

She hesitates. Makes a slight move to leave. Then stops.

Off you go. I've no further need of you.

Poopay (*cautiously*) I might sign. If I was allowed to read it first, I might.

Reece You want to read it?

Poopay No. I don't want to read it. I only want to read it if you want me to sign it.

Reece All right, read it. I don't mind. Read it. Read it. Everyone's going to be reading it sooner or later, anyway. (*He throws the papers across the desk to her.*)

Poopay What is it?

Reece What's it look like? It's a confession.

Poopay (*incredulously*) A confession? Your confession?

Reece You know you remind me of Rachel.

Poopay Rachel?

Reece My daughter Rachel. Haven't seen her for twenty years. You look very like her.

Poopay (*unimpressed*) Yes, well, I always remind people of someone.

Reece Same – hair. Same . . .

Poopay Getting back to this confession. Why were you hiding it, then? I mean, if you want to confess, why are you hiding it?

Reece It implicates – other people. That's why. Who aren't as anxious to confess as I am.

Poopay Oh. So why are you and not them?

Reece Because they're not dying and I am.

Poopay You don't know that for certain.

Reece I hope so. I've wasted a lot of money on some very expensive doctors, otherwise.

Poopay How long you got then?

Reece Few weeks, few days. They think.

Poopay Oh. I'm sorry.

Reece No, you're not. Read that and you won't be.

Poopay What have you done?

Reece I've made a great deal of money at other people's expense.

Poopay Well, that's not –

Reece At the cost of other people's lives. And I didn't give a damn.

Poopay People doing that all the time. Join the club.

Reece Not on my scale. Not juggling with currencies and creating bankruptcies, gambling with commodities and causing famines, profiting from arms deals and bringing

13

death. My second wife was absolutely right, you know. It'll all catch up with you one day, she said. You can sit there now, she said, like the cat who's swallowed the vat – but one day, there'll be a reckoning. Ruella was right. As always.

Poopay Your second wife said this?

Reece Ruella. Beautiful woman. Beautiful mind . . . A really good person, you know. Honest through and through.

Poopay What happened to her?

Reece I murdered her.

Poopay (*taking this in*) You – murdered your wife?

Reece No. Not personally. I – wanted her – dead – somebody else killed her. In this very hotel. He pushed her out of those windows. Poor bloody woman half asleep and he throws her out of the window –

Poopay Who? Who threw her?

Reece What does it matter who? I was the one responsible. He only did it because in my heart I wanted it to happen. Needed it to happen. And he knew it.

Poopay But why? Why kill your wife?

Reece Why do you kill anyone? She was in the way. She got in the way. She had to go. She was blocking up the system, threatening to foul up the machine. She found out – she wanted to tell everyone. She was an honest woman. I tell you, there's no place in business these days for a good, honest wife.

Poopay She was your second wife?

Reece Yes.

Poopay I don't like to ask really but what –

Reece He murdered her as well.

Poopay Oh, God.

Reece He drowned her. She was swimming, he held her under by her hair . . .

Poopay I hope you're mad. Because I'd hate this to be true. I really just hope you're mad. Or senile. Why didn't you stop any of this if you knew he was . . . ? You could have stopped him surely?

Reece I didn't know at the time. Of course I didn't. (*reflecting*) No. Correction. Of course I knew. I just preferred the facts as they appeared. As they suited me. Two convenient accidents that just happened to occur at absolutely the right time for me, for my career. In the end, you can always convince yourself that a version of the truth is the truth itself.

Poopay What made you change your mind?

Reece Hard facts. Like the drunken bastard standing in front of me in this very room. Swilling my whisky and telling me to my face . . .

Poopay What bastard?

Reece (*getting agitated now*) Less than a week ago. Laughing . . .

Poopay Who?

Reece Come on, old boy. Over 30 years ago – Jessica. Forget about it. All over. But Jessica hasn't forgotten, has she? August the 15th, 1981. She remembers it well enough. Swimming in Corsica . . . Aged 32. That's all she was – 32. RIP. Do you know where I was when that happened? Very conveniently?

Poopay I've no idea.

Reece Have a guess, Rachel. Go on. Taiwan. Swindling a load of poor bloody Chinamen.

Poopay (*getting alarmed for his state of health*) Steady now . . .

Reece Ruella . . . my second wife . . . Ruella. 5 October 1994. You see, I still remember exact dates . . .

Poopay You would.

Reece Accidentally fell out of that sixth-floor window. Finishes up on that pavement with her nightdress round her ears for all the world to see. What way's that for a decent woman to finish her life? And where was I?

Poopay Australia?

Reece Athens.

Poopay Swindling Italians.

Reece Buying up the world's rubber supply.

Poopay Useful.

Reece Oh, he was clever, Rachel. Clever bastard.

Poopay We're back on him again, are we?

Reece If I hadn't been so busy making deals, making money, I might have seen what he was up to. My own partner, I trusted him like my brother. I never had a brother, you know. If I'd had a brother I wouldn't have had to trust *him*. Do you know what he told me? He confessed to me that he'd even killed his own mother. Smothered her. What do you think of that?

Poopay (*very shocked*) Oh, that's awful. To smother your mother . . .

Reece His own mother! He stands in front of me, in this very room, drinking my Glenfiddich. Oh yes, he says, I killed them, he says. Make no mistake, old boy, I killed them. And I'd do it all over again if needs be, old boy. And then he just laughs. He laughs and laughs and laughs. I've never seen him laugh like that – He's mad, you know – barking mad. But I couldn't have done it without him, you see, Rachel. I'm like Faust. You ever heard of Faust, Rachel? You must have done. That's me. Sold my soul to the devil. That devil.

Poopay (*quietly*) Excuse me. Excuse me for interrupting. This is driving me mad. Would you please tell me who we are talking about here?

Reece J. S. Goodman, woman – who else?

Poopay Who the hell's J. S. Goodman?

Reece It's all in there. Read it for yourself. You still want to read it?

Poopay I think I've heard it.

Reece Then sign it. Please sign it, Rachel. Please, Rachel . . .

Poopay No, I'm not Rachel . . . My name's Poopay.

Reece Rachel?

Poopay It's French for doll. La Poupée. La poupée est dans la joujou. Merci. I'll sign it, don't worry. Give us the pen.

Reece You're a fine girl, Rachel. I love you, you know.

Poopay (*taking the pen and examining the document*) Yes . . .

Reece (*stroking her hair*) I've always loved you . . .

Poopay (*not noticing, studying the document*) Yes, that's nice . . .

17

Reece I didn't mean to kill your mother. I didn't mean to.

Poopay Then why did you, then?

Reece I needed her money, Rachel. We needed her money to save the firm.

Poopay You and J. S. Goodman. I'm signing here, all right?

Reece Thank you, Rachel. Bless you, darling. You've got your mother's hair, you know.

Poopay Depends who they sold it to. Who's this other signature? Quentin Jerkin?

Reece Quentin. That's the bellboy.

Poopay Only this place would have a bellboy called Quentin.

Reece He's a good boy, Quentin, but I couldn't trust him with this. Not with the errand.

Poopay (*alarmed*) Errand? What errand?

Reece You deliver this, in person, to my lawyer's office. Whitworth, Constable, Grady & Such.

Poopay Lawyers? Oh, now wait. Hold on . . .

Reece It's written on the front there. Constable, Grady, Such . . . Whitworth . . . See? But it's only to be delivered to a certain person. Not Bill Whitworth. For God's sake not Whitworth.

Poopay Not Whitworth?

Reece He's in with Goodman, I'm certain he is. And forget John Constable, he's too thick with Bill Whitworth . . .

Poopay Forget Constable, right. What about Grady?

Reece No, no, Grady's been dead for years. No use at all.

Poopay Right, no use whatsoever.

Reece The man you want is A. P. Such. Straight as a die. Can you remember that name, Rachel? Tony Such. Tall with dark hair and a . . .

Poopay Look, I can't do this. I really can't . . .

Reece Rachel, please . . .

Poopay I am not Rachel! And I'm not getting involved. I'm sorry. I mean, if these people are happy to push women out of windows, what chance have I got? Most of your lawyers are bent as well, from the sound of it. I'm not having anything more to do with it, I'm sorry. You'll have to ask Quentin. Ask Rachel. You can leave me out.

Reece (*half rising*) Rachel! You must . . .

Poopay Ask Lennox. Anyone but me. I'm sorry. I'm getting my coat. No charge, all right . . .

Reece Rachel . . . Please, Rachel . . . (*He grabs on to her.*)

Poopay For the last time will you stop keep calling me that? My name's not Rachel. It is Poopay Dayseer. Now, let go of me, will you . . .?

Reece (*imploringly*) Please, Rachel, I beg you. Please.

Poopay Get off! Off! Off! All right? Or I'll break your stupid fingers. (*She prises him off her.*) That's better!

> *She starts to move away. The exertion has proved too much for Reece. He collapses, making strangulated noises.*

Reece (*choking*) Rach . . . Ra . . . Ra . . . el . . . el . . . el . . .

Poopay What you doing, now? What is it? What's the matter?

Reece Ra . . . eeelll . . . !

Poopay What's the matter with you . . . ?

Reece lies on the floor making strangled breathing sounds.

Oh, my God! Oh, God! I'm getting out of here. I'm sorry, I'm getting out.

She runs into the bedroom. Reece continues to lie there choking. Banging of cupboards from the bedroom.

(*off, in a panic*) Where's my coat? What's he done with my bloody coat?

Further banging. Poopay returns with her coat. She starts putting it on.

Look, I'm sorry about this. I'm making no charge. All right?

Reece (*weakly*) Rachel . . .

Poopay (*grabbing her bag*) That was on the house. I hope you're better soon . . .

Reece (*gasping*) Rachel . . . please . . . help me . . .

Poopay (*hesitating, then relenting*) Oh, God. All right. Wait. (*She puts down her bag and picks up the phone. She consults the notepad and works the phone.*) I'll phone him. I'll phone your – your butler – whatever he is – Then I'm away, all right? (*into phone*) Hallo . . . is that . . . whoeveritis? . . . This is Poopay . . . the – specialist consultant . . . in room – hang on a minute . . . (*she studies the phone*) . . . What? . . . No, he's not – he's lying on the floor . . . he's had some sort of . . . hallo . . . (*The phone has gone dead.*)

Poopay replaces the receiver and grabs up her bag. Reece continues to lie on the floor, breathing with apparent difficulty.

(*to Reece, loudly*) There's somebody coming. Can you hear me? There's somebody on their way. You'll be OK now.

Reece groans.

Oh, soddit. Here.

She grabs a cushion from the sofa and puts it under Reece's head.

(*as she does this*) I'm S&M, not doctors and bloody nurses . . . Right. Better? 'Night 'night.

She takes up her bag once more and heads for the front door. Just as she reaches it, the door opens and Julian steps into the room.

Julian Where are you off to?

Poopay He's there. I've done what I can . . .

Julian Just a minute. What have you done to him?

Poopay He's all yours. Good night.

Julian kneels beside Reece, concerned.

Julian Reece? What's she done? What have you done to him, you slag?

Poopay I haven't done nothing. Good night. (*She makes to go out of the door.*)

Julian Hey!

Poopay What?

Julian You're not going anywhere.

Poopay Who says so?

Julian I do.

Poopay Oh yes? You and who else?

Julian Me and those two gentlemen down the hall there for starters.

Poopay takes a look down the hall and looks uncertain.

Now kindly step back inside, please.

Poopay (*doing so*) I can call for assistance, you know. If necessary.

Julian Give me a hand with him. If you've damaged him I will personally pull your head off.

Poopay and Julian lift Reece off the floor with difficulty.

Gently! Gently!

Poopay (*as they do this*) You keep threatening me, I can easily summon the management, you know.

Julian I wouldn't bother, we own the hotel.

Poopay (*realizing she is in deep*) Oh. Do you?

Reece groans.

Julian (*to Reece*) All right, old lad . . . Easy. Easy.

They disappear momentarily into the bedroom.

(*off*) Down here.

Poopay (*off*) Right. (*She returns.*) I'll be off then, all right?

Julian (*returning swiftly*) Hey! I said wait a minute . . .

Poopay Yes, well, I've done . . .

Julian Sit down.

Poopay I've done what I can –

Julian Sit!

Poopay sits.

You go when I tell you you can go. All right? Take your coat off. Relax.

He picks up the phone and punches a number. Poopay removes her coat, reluctantly.

It's Julian. Get Doctor Joachim . . . Yes. Yes, he's had another one . . . Yes. It's in my book. Right. Quickly.

Julian hangs up. He turns to Poopay.

Poopay (*rather nervous*) I don't think you really need me here any more, do you? I think I'll –

Julian So. What happened?

Poopay How do you mean?

Julian I mean with him. What happened to my friend Mr Welles?

Poopay Nothing. We were –

Julian Playing little games with him, were you? Showing off your bag of tricks? (*He kicks her bag.*)

Poopay No. We were just –

Julian Just what?

Poopay Talking.

Julian Talking?

Poopay And then he – sort of fell over.

Julian While you were talking?

Poopay Yes.

Julian You must have a very forceful line in conversation.

Poopay Not really.

Julian What were you talking about?

Poopay is trying to keep her eyes off the confession on the desk.

Poopay Nothing.

Julian picks up the cushion from the floor. He starts to toss it from hand to hand. Poopay becomes riveted by this.

Julian I'll repeat that question just once more. What were you both talking about?

Poopay (*a bit croakily*) I can't remember.

Julian You can't remember?

Poopay No.

Julian You can't remember a conversation you were holding less than five minutes ago? Suffer from memory loss, do you?

Poopay doesn't answer.

Well, do you? You know what is sometimes a good cure for memory loss? Shock. You give the person a shock. It sometimes serves to jolt the memory. As you might do any piece of faulty equipment. Like that.

He bangs the cushion suddenly and throws it quite sharply on to the sofa beside Poopay. She jumps.

One more time, then? What were you both talking about?

Poopay's eyes stray momentarily back to the desk. Julian intercepts her look this time. Poopay seizes her opportunity to try and make a bolt for it.

(*going to the desk*) What's this then? Is this what all the excitement was – SIT DOWN!

Poopay sits again, swiftly. Julian picks up the document and skims through it. Through the window, the distant sound of automatic gun fire. Poopay and Julian both react. Julian moves to the window.

'S'alright. Other side of the river. Deptford, I think. (*He resumes reading.*) Oh, yes. Oh, yes. I had some small inkling this was on the cards. I'm going to have to keep a closer eye on him for the remainder of his days. He's becoming a liability, the wicked old thing. Nothing like imminent death, is there, for bringing out a guilty conscience. Wouldn't you agree?

Poopay (*huskily*) I wouldn't know.

Julian Did you read this?

Poopay shakes her head.

No?

Poopay No. Not a single word.

Julian studies her.

Julian You signed it though, didn't you? This is your name, I take it? Poopay Dog-ear, is it? Oh, yes. And here's our old pal Quentin. Must have a word with him, too. And you say you haven't read it?

No reply.

Then you might as well read it now, hadn't you?

He throws the document into her lap.

Poopay No, thank you.

Julian That's entirely up to you. Since I don't believe you, there's no way you're going to leave here alive in either event, is there?

Poopay suddenly makes a bolt for it. She throws her coat at Julian which he catches without difficulty. But it allows her the split second required to bolt across the

*room and into the bathroom where she slams the door
behind her and locks it. Julian is only seconds behind
her, still holding her coat.*

Oh, now that's silly. That is silly. That is very, very silly,
isn't it? Now you're going to make me cross.

*He stands for a moment, then moves swiftly across the
room towards the bedroom door. He stops briefly, picks
up her bag and takes it with him into the bedroom.
Meanwhile Poopay looks around her and finds she still
has the confession in her hands. Deciding the best
course is to get rid of it, she kneels and hides it back in
the bidet as before. She gets back on her feet and for the
first time sees there is another door to the bathroom. She
moves to it hastily to lock it, but Julian is there before
her. He moves into the room. He still holds her bag. She
backs away until she reaches the bidet. She loses her
balance and sits. Julian stands over her.*

Poopay We can talk about this. There's no need . . . I
mean, I'm not going to . . .

Julian opens her bag.

Julian Got quite a collection in here, haven't you?
Handcuffs. Whips. Cat-o'-nine-tails. The things a girl
carries in her handbag these days. What is all this junk?

Poopay I'm a . . . I'm a . . . I'm . . .

Julian You're a what? What precisely are you?

Poopay (*in a tiny voice*) I'm a dominatrix . . .

Julian Are you now? Well, you certainly scare the hell out
of me.

Poopay Is that what you'd like? I mean, if that's . . . I'd be
very happy to . . . I mean, free . . . no charge . . .

Julian I wouldn't touch you with a lavatory brush, you grimy little woman . . .

Poopay Yes, well, just as you like.

Julian What we're in need of here, correct me if I'm wrong, dominatrix, is something in the nature of a tragedy. Elderly gentleman, distinguished businessman, pillar of society, rents the services of a whip woman, together with all her deviant commodities – (*He tosses the bag back through the bedroom door.*) Leaving her client helpless as a turkey, she comes into the bathroom – to see if there's anything worth taking. Drugs maybe? Yes. She opens the bathroom cabinet . . . (*He does so.*) . . . in search of something to give her a bit of a buzz, get her dull little brain working and, yes, she finds this . . . looks interesting, doesn't it? . . . which she swallows in one gulp. (*He holds up a small bottle.*) Not bothering to read, in her excitement, on the back: (*reading*) 'Caution. Dangerous to exceed the stated dose.' Oh, dear, what an oversight. Which, of course, taken on top of these pills – (*taking up a bottle of pills*) – that the greedy girl had already gobbled up, resulted in her sad demise. That should do it, shouldn't it?

He unscrews the bottle top, then the pill bottle. He pours a few pills into the palm of his hand. He takes up the open medicine bottle with the other. Poopay watches him with horrified fascination.

We have a choice now. This can be voluntary – or this can be compulsory. It's entirely up to you.

Poopay You – you – you could go to prison for this, you know . . .

Julian stares at her, startled. Suddenly he starts to laugh. Long and hard. It isn't a cheering sound. The laughter stops, eventually.

27

(*in a near whisper*) Oh, dear God you're him, aren't you? Him. You're J. S. Goodman?

Julian Julian to my closest friends. (*extending his hands*) Come on then. Come on. Good girl.

  Poopay draws back.

No? All right. It has to be the hard way, then.

Poopay (*a last bid*) You do this you'll never get it back, will you? His confession. The pieces of paper he signed. You kill me, you'll never find them.

Julian (*slowly*) Where is it? (*louder*) Where is it? (*savagely*) WHERE IS IT?

  Julian switches the bottle to the hand which holds the pills and swiftly lunges out and grabs Poopay by her hair. He drags her towards him. Poopay's wig comes away in his hand. Julian is again momentarily startled. Poopay makes a dart through the bedroom door.

(*angrily*) Come here! (*with a cry*) Mother! Come here, Mother!

Poopay (*as she runs*) Mother?

  Julian initially chases after her into the bedroom. Poopay re-emerges immediately through the other bedroom door into the sitting room, literally running for her life. She makes first for the front door, opens it, remembers and then closes it again. She looks around and makes a dart for the only other remaining door in the room, the communicating door. During this, Julian re-emerges from the bedroom back into the bathroom, doubling back to cut her off. He has discarded her wig and the drugs he was holding. He goes to open the bathroom door leading to the sitting room. It is still locked from when Poopay locked it earlier and this

28

*momentarily delays him. Julian fumbles with the lock,
cursing. All this allows time for Poopay to step inside
the linking lobby and shut the door behind her. She
stands blinking and breathless in the confined, dark
space. Julian, who has been hot on her heels, tries the
door handle but Poopay's body wedges it shut. He finds
he is suddenly short of breath.*

Julian (*to himself*) I'm getting too old for this, Mother. (*to
Poopay, through the door*) You can stay locked in there as
long as you like. You can't go anywhere, you know. That
just links with the room next door, that's all. Just a store
room in there. No way out. Just a great big cupboard.
(*rattling the handle*) Come on. Come on out. You might as
well.

The doorbell chimes. Julian curses under his breath.

I can wait. I'll be waiting for you. Don't worry.

*Julian looks round and makes one or two rapid
decisions. Change of plan. He takes up Poopay's coat
from the floor and goes out through the bathroom,
closing the bathroom cabinet as he goes.
The doorbell chimes again.*

(*yelling*) All right. I'm coming, I'm coming. Keep it down,
will you, there's a dying man in here . . .

*Julian disappears into the bedroom.
Poopay, alone in her cupboard, tries the other door. It
opens. As it does so, the unit revolves so that she,
effectively, steps back into the same area she has left.
We are in the same place but we have moved in time.
Back twenty years. It is 1994.
Poopay peers around, accustoming her eyes to the
gloom. She starts to creep across the room. She falls
over something.*

Poopay Ow! Ooh! Ow!

Ruella (*from the bedroom*) Who is that? Who's out there?

> *Poopay freezes.*

Who's there?

> *Poopay hurries back to the cupboard but has trouble locating it. Before she can, the sitting room lights come on and* **Ruella** *is standing in the bedroom doorway in her nightdress. At forty-five, she is a handsome, elegant woman – the sort other women often aspire to be like – capable and determined and, as described by Reece, with a fierce sense of fairness, honesty and justice. At present she is fairly angry at the intrusion.*

Who the hell are you?

Poopay (*confused*) I'm sorry, I . . . I'm . . . (*She is rapidly going to pieces.*)

Ruella What are you doing here? This is my room . . .

Poopay I'm so sorry. I thought it was a cupboard.

Ruella A what?

Poopay A cupboard. I was informed it was a cupboard. I'm so sorry.

Ruella It's my room.

Poopay Yes.

Ruella Mine. Why did you think it was a cupboard? Were you looking for a cupboard? Why do you want a cupboard?

Poopay I don't want a cupboard, I was trying to . . .

Ruella Why are you dressed like that? Are you in fancy dress?

Poopay (*her teeth chattering*) No, no I'm a dom . . . I'm a dom . . .

Ruella You're a what?

Poopay I'm a dominatrix . . .

Ruella A dominatrix?

Poopay Yes.

Ruella I don't even know what that is, I'm sorry. Something sexual, isn't it?

Poopay whimpers.

Well, you can't do it in here, whatever it is. Are you on drugs or something?

Another whimper from Poopay.

Would you kindly leave my room at once or I shall phone security.

Poopay (*weakly*) No . . . no . . .

Ruella What do you mean, no? Get out at once. It's nearly midnight. I want to get some sleep. I have – mountains to do in the morning.

Poopay They're waiting out there.

Ruella Out where?

Poopay There.

Ruella What, outside my room? How many more of you are there?

Ruella crosses and opens the door. She takes a swift look up and down the hall. As she does so, Poopay draws back into the corner of the room, terrified.

Poopay (*terrified*) No . . .

Ruella (*closing the door*) Well, there's nothing out there except dirty shoes.

Poopay cowers, shivering, making whimpering noises.

You're obviously on something appalling. You're quite evidently hallucinating. Well, there's nothing I can do. I'm phoning security.

Poopay (*a great cry*) NO!!!

Ruella (*fiercely*) Will you keep your voice down? There are people in this hotel who are trying to sleep. For goodness sake have some consideration for others. What's the matter with you? You ought to be ashamed of yourself. Now, sit down there and be quiet, this minute. Pull yourself together, you're a grown woman.

Poopay, not for the first time this evening, sits meekly as she is told. Ruella lifts the phone and punches 0.

(*into phone*) Hallo. This is suite 647. I've just been woken up by a woman who's broken in here. She appears to be high on drugs and dressed in rubber . . .

Poopay Leather.

Ruella What? Leather, then. Dressed in leather. Will you please come and remove her at once. . . . Thank you . . . yes, 647. Mrs Welles. And this is not what I expect from a five-star hotel. (*She hangs up.*)

Poopay Mrs Welles? You're Mrs Welles?

Ruella Yes.

Poopay Are you married to Mr Welles?

Ruella Yes. Amazingly. Currently. Though I don't suspect for very much longer – anyway, what's it got to do with you? Mind you own business.

Poopay The Mr Welles who owns this hotel? The Mr Welles in the room next door?

Ruella Next door?

Poopay Through there. Through that door.

Ruella Certainly not. My husband's abroad, at present. And he certainly doesn't own this hotel and if he did, I'd advise him to sell it immediately. Anyway there's no room next door. Not that way. It's a box room or something. I checked on the map there. I always check my fire exits. Most of these places are death traps.

Poopay It's not, there's a suite through there. It's a great big suite like this one. (*starting to cry*) I promise. Please, believe me.

Ruella (*more gently*) Listen. Just try and calm down. Sit there quietly and take deep breaths, all right.

Poopay does as she's told.

That's it. Not too fast. Slowly. Slowly. Now, what's your name?

Poopay Poopay.

Ruella Poopay? Is that your real name? It can't possibly be.

Poopay No.

Ruella What's your proper name, then?

Poopay Phoebe.

Ruella Phoebe? Oh, that's much nicer.

Poopay I hate it.

Ruella Well, you shouldn't. It's a very fine name. Phoebe was a goddess. Did you know that?

Poopay Was she?

Ruella Oh, yes. A very important one. The sister of Apollo, the sun god. Can't get much more important than that, can you? You should be proud of it, Phoebe. Mind you, I don't know what she'd think if she saw you looking like this.

Poopay You're positive there's no suite next door? You're sure?

Ruella It's just a store room, I promise you. Do you want to look? I don't even know if it's open. (*She moves to try the door.*)

Poopay (*alarmed again*) No, don't open that door. Please . . .

Ruella All right, all right . . . Something's really terrified you, hasn't it? What is it? Tell me. I'll listen.

Poopay He tried to kill me.

Ruella Who did? Who tried to kill you?

Poopay J. S. Goodman.

Ruella J. S. – ? You mean *Julian* Goodman?

Poopay Julian, yes. Julian Goodman. Do you know him?

Ruella Yes, of course I do. He's my husband's business partner.

Poopay Your husband?

Ruella My husband, Reece. Reece Welles.

Poopay Then it is him, that is him.

Ruella What?

Poopay The old man next door. Your husband, the man who's just collapsed.

Ruella (*patiently*) We'll try again, shall we? My husband is indeed Reece Welles but he is not staying in this hotel. (*As she speaks she goes into the bedroom briefly and returns, pulling on her dressing gown.*) He is not due back till tomorrow in time for lunch. A final attempt, on his side anyway, at a last-minute reconciliation; but as far as I'm concerned, far too late. I've stuck it for twelve years but enough is quite sufficient. I don't know what your involvement is with Reece, dear, and I really don't want to know, but as from tomorrow you're welcome to him. Though you may have to visit him in jail, I warn you.

Poopay No, you don't understand, he's –

Ruella Incidentally, in your book he may be an old man. But as far as I'm concerned he's still a comparatively young man of fifty. That spoken by a comparatively young woman of forty-five.

Poopay Fifty? He can't be fifty? He's –

Ruella As for Julian, I'm on less sure ground, I must say. He's a perfectly despicable man and I wouldn't put anything past him.

Poopay He killed his own mother . . .

Ruella From my knowledge of Julian that is just possible. My husband's infatuated with him. In his eyes, Julian can do no wrong. Which is one of the reasons I'm leaving, if you must know. It was either Julian or me. I don't know how long they thought they'd get away with it. If they imagined I was just going to stand by and let them embezzle millions.

Poopay My God. I've just – I've just . . . What's your name? No, wait. I'll tell you your name. Not Jessica – that was the first one. It's Rue – Rue . . .

Ruella Ruella.

Poopay Ruella, yes. You're right . . .

Ruella I thought I was.

Poopay He must have got it all confused, you see. Your husband. He thought I was his daughter Rachel, you see. He was all muddled up. He said he'd killed Jessica and then he'd killed you . . .

Ruella Reece said that?

Poopay Yes. Only he got it muddled. He means to kill you, only he hasn't yet.

Ruella He's in Greece.

Poopay Greece, yes. Greece. Buying up all the rubber. Only he can't be in Greece, can he? He's next door. Only he can't be next door because he has to be in Greece for Julian to kill you, you see . . .

Ruella Julian? Julian's killing me as well?

Poopay No, not as well. Julian's the one who's going to do it, you see. He's planning to throw you out of a hotel window. The one next door. While Reece is in Greece.

Ruella (*staring at her*) I think you're the one that's muddled, not my husband. Deep breaths now, deep breaths. Head between your knees . . .

Ruella gently but firmly pushes Poopay's head down between her knees.

That's it. Deep breath as you come up. And down – and let it all out – that's it. (*conversationally, like a hairdresser*) So, what's it like being a prostitute? Is it fun?

Poopay (*as she comes up*) Not very, no.

Ruella And what do you do when you're dominatrixing? Is that hard work? Keep breathing . . .

36

Poopay It's all right, you know, it's a bit more interesting than straight work –

Ruella And what do you have to do exactly?

Poopay Oh you know, beat people, tie them up, you know . . .

Ruella That doesn't sound very life enhancing, does it – ?

Poopay They seem to like it . . .

Ruella Yes, well, some people like listening to Schoenberg but I don't think it's to be encouraged . . .

The doorbell chimes.

Ah, here we are.

Ruella moves to the door. Poopay cowers and moans.

(*soothingly*) Now it's all right, it's all right. It's just the house detective. (*calling through the door*) Hallo?

Harold (*from outside*) Security. Harold Palmer.

Ruella (*to Poopay*) Security. There we are. (*opening the door*) Come in.

Harold, *the house detective, enters. A lugubrious man who's seen it all several times over. He is currently fifty-five years old.*

Harold Evening, Mrs Welles. Sorry about this. They sometimes slip past you. (*seeing Poopay*) Dear, oh dear, where did you spring from then? Walk in here like that, did you? I don't know, it gets worse, you know. Come on, up you get. I'll take you down the service lift. Not going through the foyer like that. Frighten the night porter.

Ruella Be gentle with her. She's had some sort of shock.

Harold Caught sight of herself in the mirror probably.

Poopay Shut your face . . .

Harold Hey, hey, hey . . .

Ruella Listen, I'll lend you my mac. But you must give it back. I'm going to trust you. Will you promise?

Poopay Thank you. I promise.

Ruella goes into the bedroom momentarily.

Harold No need for that, Mrs Welles, I'll find something. Throw a bit of polythene over her or something. Don't want to dirty your coat.

Poopay Look, stuff up, all right?

Harold Now you watch that language. This is a respectable hotel.

Poopay Respectable?

Ruella returns with a raincoat.

Ruella Here we are.

Poopay (*starting to put on the coat*) That's a good one. Try telling that to Lennox . . .

Harold Lennox? Who's Lennox?

Poopay Your pimping, poncing, poxy head porter. That Lennox. (*to Ruella*) Thank you very much.

Harold Lennox? Head porter's name's George.

Poopay George? Where have you been? Wake up. George's dead, isn't he?

Harold Dead? No, he just looks it.

Poopay George died ages ago. 'bout eight years. Got run over by a taxi. Where have you been? Asleep?

Harold Come on. This way. And I'm having a polaroid of you before you go. No way you're getting back in here.

Poopay (*ignoring Harold, to Ruella*) Goodbye. Thank you very much, you've been very kind. Just – I know you think I'm mad – but be careful, will you? Be very, very careful.

Harold Come on . . .

Poopay (*indicating the communicating door*) And keep away from that door. Whatever you do. He's only the other side. All right?

Harold (*tugging her out*) This is your last warning.

Poopay Yes, OK. Don't pull me.

Ruella (*something is troubling her*) Just a minute – Harold – it is, Harold, isn't it?

Harold That's right, madam. Harold Palmer.

Ruella Phoebe . . .

Poopay Yes?

Harold (*scornfully*) Phoebe?

Ruella What happened to Jessica, can you remember? How did she die?

Poopay She was drowned. In – wait – yes, 1981. Year I was born. Swimming in Corsica. Aged thirty-two. Something like that. It was supposed to be an accident. But it wasn't. He held her down. By the hair.

Ruella (*rather shaken*) I see.

Harold That's it. Come on then, Phoebe. (*laughing*) Phoebe . . .

Poopay (*as she's dragged away*) See what I mean . . .

Ruella You stick with it, girl. Stick with Phoebe.

*The door closes on Harold and Poopay. Ruella stands
thoughtfully. She shakes her head.*

(*to herself*) Year she was born? She may want to lie about
her age but she'll never get away with thirteen.

*She makes a move to the communicating door, changes
her mind and then moves to the bedroom. She is about
to go in and switch off the lights, when she hesitates.
She returns to the communicating door, her hand on the
handle, deliberating.*

Ridiculous. Quite absurd. Still, I won't sleep otherwise,
will I?

*Cautiously she opens the first door, steps inside the
lobby and finds that she needs to close it before she can
open the other door.*

(*standing in the confined space, quietly*) Help.

*The unit revolves as before. Ruella opens the second
door to arrive back in the suite. It is now in darkness.
Time has changed yet again. It is now 1974.*

(*staring into the darkness*) Odd sort of box room.

*Ruella moves further into the room groping round
furniture. From the bedroom the sound of girlish giggles
and manly growls. Honeymooners having fun in the
dark.*

Oh, no. Not in the box room, surely . . . They're
everywhere.

*She starts to try and retrace her steps. It's difficult.
Before she's gone far, a young woman comes out of the
bedroom. It is Jessica, a young bride of twenty-five, rich,
pretty and vivacious.*

Jessica (*calling to someone in the bedroom, giggling*) . . . I

need to go. I have to go. I'm sorry, I'm bursting . . .
Sorry . . .

Reece (*off, from the bedroom*) You're going the wrong
way . . .

Jessica (*calling*) What's that?

Reece (*off*) The bathroom's the other way.

Jessica Oh, where am I? I'm lost, I'm lost. Where's the
loo? I need the loooo . . .

Reece (*coming out of the bedroom*) Just a minute, here
you are, you . . .

> *The room is flooded with light as Reece switches them
> on. He and Jessica are both near naked. Fortunately,
> Reece is carrying a sheet which they both clasp to
> themselves in one lightning movement as they see Ruella.*

Jessica (*squawking with surprise*) Oh!

Reece (*likewise*) Ah!

> *Reece is now thirty.*
>   *They stare at Ruella. Ruella stares at them. A shocked
> silence.*

How did you get in here? This is a private room.

Jessica (*echoing him*) . . . private room.

Reece Get out at once.

Jessica Get out.

Ruella (*still stunned*) I'm sorry, I . . .

Jessica How dare you!

Reece How dare you!

Ruella (*wonderingly*) Reece?

Reece (*startled*) What?

Ruella Jessica?

Jessica (*equally startled*) Yes?

Reece Look, I don't know who you are but –

Ruella (*confused*) Yes, I'm sorry. I'm going, I'm going. I'm going now. I'm sorry.

Ruella, in panic, opens the communicating door and steps back into the lobby closing the door behind her.

Reece No, not that way . . .

He darts forward to reveal he is just in his shorts. He tries to follow Ruella but finds the door won't open.
  Ruella stands for a second in the lobby area, recovering from the shock.

Honestly. What a damn cheek.

Jessica Do you know her?

Reece Of course I don't. Never seen her before in my life.

Jessica She seemed to know you. She knew your name.

Reece She knew your name, come to that.

Jessica Yes. How odd. Weird.

Reece Come on. You'll get cold . . .

Jessica (*as they go back into the bedroom*) I still need the loo . . .

Reece turns off the lights.

Reece (*following her*) Then go to the loo . . .

Jessica (*off*) I'm not going in there on my own. Not now . . .

*Ruella has recovered sufficiently to open the further
door. The unit revolves. She opens the door rather
slowly.*

*She is back in her old room where the lights are on, as
before.*

*Her phone starts ringing. She runs to answer it,
closing the communicating door behind her.*

Ruella Hallo . . . Harold? . . . Who? Phoebe? . . . Has
she? No, let her come up. No . . . Yes . . . Yes, of course I
am . . . Straightaway . . . (*She hangs up. Still not fully
recovered from her shock*) Oh. Oh–oh–oh.

*She goes to the sideboard unit and opens it, to reveal a
mini-bar. She takes out a miniature brandy, locates a
glass on the shelf and pours the lot into it. She tosses the
bottle in the waste bin and downs the drink in one. Her
eyes water. She is about to have a second one when the
doorbell chimes. Ruella goes to the front door.*

Hallo?

Harold (*outside the door*) Security . . . Harold Palmer.

*Ruella pulls open the door hastily to admit a distraught
Poopay with Harold close behind her.*

Ruella Come in, come in. Thank you so much, Harold.

She lets Poopay inside.

Harold I hope you know what you're doing, Mrs Welles.

Ruella Thank you so much.

Harold You want me to stay, keep an eye on her?

Ruella No, Harold, it's perfectly all right. There's no need
for that.

Harold Well, I'll be downstairs. Give me a bell when
you've finished with her. I'll take her down again. She's in

a very unstable condition, if you ask me. (*to Poopay*) Any more trouble, it's the police next time. All right, girl?

Ruella (*easing him out of the door*) Thank you, Harold.

Ruella closes the door and turns to Poopay.

Poopay (*looking at her*) I'm glad to see you.

Ruella (*embracing her, impetuously*) It's good to see you.

Poopay responds. They cling on for a moment. Two women in need of mutual support.

Poopay (*the first to recover*) I've just been out there. I don't know what's happening. My flat's gone.

Ruella Gone?

Poopay (*her teeth chattering*) It isn't there any more. It's vanished. Not just my flat. The whole bloody building. They can't just have taken it away, can they? Knocked it down since half past eight this evening? It's not possible.

Ruella You sure you didn't have the wrong street? You were very upset, you –

Reece No! I didn't. I know where I live, for God's sake. It can't have gone. I mean it was an official, you know, hostel. You know.

Ruella No.

Poopay You know. State-controlled. Official, not private.

Ruella Just a minute. Have a drink. You need a drink.

Poopay Yes, please.

Ruella raids the mini-bar again.

They closed the Virtuality Centre as well.

Ruella The what?

Poopay Opened a video shop instead. Video shop, I ask you. I haven't seen one of them for years. Who the hell even owns a video these days?

Ruella Brandy or whisky?

Poopay Whisky'll do.

Ruella Now, we've both got to sit down, keep calm and try and put it all together. Here. (*She gives a glass to Poopay.*)

Poopay Ta.

Ruella There is nothing happening here that cannot be explained logically.

Poopay (*sceptically*) Oh, yes?

Ruella Even if the logic is – in this instance – unfamiliar logic.

Poopay I'm lost already. (*raising her glass*) Shine.

Ruella Yes. Cheers.

  They drink. Ruella warms to her task.

Firstly, I ought to tell you that I've been next door myself.

Poopay Through there?

Ruella Yes.

Poopay Was he still there? Did you see him?

Ruella Julian? No, I didn't. I did see my husband, though.

Poopay How is he? Is he any better?

Ruella Very well. Terribly well in fact. Having a high old time.

Poopay Must have a good doctor. He was dying the last time I saw him.

Ruella Tell me something, Phoebe. What age would you say he was? Reece.

Poopay Oh, I don't know. Seventy? Seventy-five?

Ruella No younger?

Poopay Shouldn't have thought so.

Ruella Certainly not, say, in his twenties?

Poopay In his twenties?

Ruella Yes.

Poopay Not unless he's had a hell of a childhood. What is all this?

Ruella You see, I think the Reece that I saw just now . . . isn't necessarily the Reece that you saw.

Poopay It wasn't?

Ruella No. Not even the Reece that I know now.

Poopay (*indicating Ruella's glass*) You've had a few of them, haven't you?

Ruella You want another?

Poopay I think one of us ought to stay sober.

Ruella (*a sudden stab*) Phoebe, what year do you think it is now?

Poopay Year?

Ruella What's the date? For you?

Poopay For me? (*trying to remember*) Well, for me it's July twenty – ? 25th, is it today?

Ruella July?

Poopay Yes.

Ruella And the year?

Poopay The year – surprise – is 2014 – look, what's this all about?

Ruella 2014?

Poopay Yes. So?

Ruella Wait there. (*She gets up and goes into the bedroom.*)

Poopay (*to herself*) I can't believe this. I'm surrounded by them.

Ruella returns with the evening paper. She tosses it to Poopay.

Ruella Take a look at that.

Poopay Oh, yes. What a good idea. Man tries to kill me. Another one nearly drops dead, someone's walked off with my flat so we might as well sit and read the paper, mightn't we?

Ruella Don't read it. Just look at the date.

Poopay The date?

Ruella Just the date.

Poopay (*glancing at the paper briefly*) Oh, yes. That's fun, isn't it?

Ruella 1994, right?

Poopay Yes, I'd have been – I'd only have been – in '94? A baby. I was tiny – very, very young. (*being honest*) Well, I was thirteen actually, but don't tell anyone. I've seen these advertised. You can get them for, like the day you were

47

born, can't you? (*Poopay has now got intrigued with the paper. She opens it at random to a fashion page. Screaming with laughter*) Hey! Hey! Look at that? You remember these? We used to wear those, didn't we? My mum did.

Ruella Phoebe!

Poopay Here. Look at this bloke. Remember him?

Ruella Yes, I do very well. Now listen –

Poopay Went to jail, didn't he?

Ruella Phoebe, now – (*intrigued*) My God, did he? Does he?

Poopay You remember that. Terrific scandal. Even I remember that . . .

Ruella No, I don't remember, that's the point –

Poopay They made a film of it with whatsisname – you know – pop singer . . .

Ruella (*loudly*) Phoebe, that is today's paper.

Poopay What?

Ruella This is today's paper. This is today's news. Look. This is today's date. Wednesday, 5 October 1994. That is when I am living. I, Ruella Welles. I am Reece's second wife who according to you is dead. Murdered. What is more, I have just ten minutes ago seen Jessica, Reece's first wife whom you and I both know to be dead – according to me as a result of an accident; according to you, again, murdered.

Poopay (*staring at her for a second*) You're dead?

Ruella In a sense.

Poopay (*putting down her glass*) I'm getting out of here.

48

Ruella Wait.

Poopay No, this is getting weird . . .

Ruella Don't you see? It's all to do with time.

Poopay Time I was going home.

Ruella Phoebe, you can't get home. Can't you see it's a –
what did they used to call it – a time warp. We're from
different times. For you it's 2014, for me it's 1994, and for
Jessica it's – whatever – it looked as if it was their
honeymoon night – when would that have been? – 1974?
Yes, that would follow – twenty-year gaps. Of course. And
somehow – across time – we've – linked. Been linked. You,
me and her.

Poopay (*stunned*) You, me and her . . .

Ruella It explains it, anyway . . .

Poopay Why should we link? What links us?

Ruella I don't know. Julian?

Poopay Julian?

Ruella Maybe he murders us all.

A silence. Quite suddenly Poopay starts screaming.
Ruella is alarmed. She grabs hold of Poopay.

(*shaking her*) Phoebe! Phoebe! Come on, now. Come on.
Pull yourself together.

Poopay (*calming down*) I'm sorry.

Ruella That's better.

Poopay Mustn't disturb the people next door, must we?

She starts laughing, somewhat uncontrollably. Ruella,
despite herself, joins in.

Ruella (*laughing*) What, the honeymooners, you mean?

Poopay (*laughing*) I was thinking more of the mother killer actually. Needs his beauty sleep.

They laugh themselves to a standstill. A slight pause. They reflect.

I can't cope with all this. I'm sorry . . . (*She starts to cry softly.*)

Ruella No, I'm sorry. That wasn't the most helpful of theories. I'm sorry. I was just – trying to look for a pattern. Something to explain why . . . Come on, now. Maybe we can change things . . .

Poopay (*crying*) We're all dead, that's what it is. We've died and gone to hell. To a hotel in hell.

Ruella I mean, things can alter. Things have already altered. You're here. That's certainly altered things for me. At least now I know I'm going to get pushed out of a window. Not a lot of help, but it's something. And as for Jessica – well, I've wrecked her wedding night, poor girl. That's a start, surely?

Poopay How can we change anything? We can't.

Ruella That's a very feeble attitude, I must say.

Poopay What will be, will be . . . Que sera –

Ruella Oh, don't be so pathetic. Come on, shape up, girl. We're going to win this. We're going to fight it, we're going to win it. Otherwise why were we given this chance, eh? Tell me that. The first thing we have to do is alert Jessica. I don't think she's in any immediate danger. If she's on her honeymoon now in '74, she didn't drown till – 1981. Gives her a good seven years. Still, she ought to be forewarned. And maybe any different action she takes – subsequently – could affect things for us. Maybe she could get him arrested. Why did they kill her, did they say?

Poopay They needed her money to save the firm.

Ruella God, how pathetic. Not even a decent *crime passionnelle*. Typical of Reece. What we need is proof, you see. To convince Jessica. It's not going to be easy. A woman wildly in love, on her honeymoon, isn't readily going to accept that her husband is planning to murder her in seven years' time.

Poopay Maybe I could dress up as a fortune teller . . .

Ruella I think you've done enough dressing up for one evening, if you don't mind my saying so. We must fit you up with some proper clothes, too. You can't turn up in the bridal suite dressed like that.

Poopay Bridal suite? I'm not going in there.

Ruella Of course you are. We do this together. Strength in numbers.

Poopay I'm not going anywhere. I want to go home.

Ruella Phoebe, you can't go home. Be sensible. If you try to go home now, you probably will die. And if you're right, I most certainly will. Now you might not care about your life but I happen to value mine a great deal and I intend to live it till I'm very, very old indeed. Now please!

Poopay I'm sorry.

Ruella All right. (*Slight pause.*) Did he – did they – mention at all when I was – when I died.

Poopay Yes. But I've forgotten. All I remember was, he was in Greece – buying rubber – and you were staying in this hotel.

Ruella Precisely as things are now?

Poopay Yes. When were you planning to check out of here?

Ruella Tomorrow morning.

Poopay And when does your husband get back?

Ruella Tomorrow morning. (*A slight pause.*) It's tonight then, isn't it? It has to be.

Poopay Unless he's planning some more trips to Greece.

Ruella Not married to me, he's not. If I have anything to do with it by tomorrow evening he'll be in prison.

Poopay And if he has anything to do with it, by tomorrow morning –

Ruella Yes, all right. Point taken, thank you.

Poopay Maybe, if you were a bit more reasonable – perhaps he'd change his mind – about murdering you.

Ruella Reasonable? Have you any idea what that man's doing? And has done? Have you any idea at all. He should have been shot. Instead, there he is cavorting around – by all accounts – seventy years old, with women in their – I'm sorry. There's just absolutely no justice.

Poopay He wasn't very happy.

Ruella Good. I'm glad to hear it.

Poopay He said he was dying.

Ruella Better still.

Poopay It wasn't him who killed you, anyway. It was Julian. He said he didn't know anything about it.

Ruella (*considering this*) No. He probably didn't. Knowing Reece. He chooses to know only what he wants to know. He never likes facing the unpleasant things in life. He's an exceptionally clever, charming man in many ways. But he leaves the difficult, the nasty things – the messy things to me or the Julians of this world. If he can't face it, it doesn't exist. If I ever dared fall ill he'd find some excuse to go away until I was better. When I was pregnant, God, I thought I'd never see him again . . .

Poopay You've got children?

Ruella One. Thomas. He's eleven. At boarding school. Brilliant boy. Quite brilliant. Did he – ? Did Reece mention him at all? Thomas?

Poopay No. Not at all.

Ruella Oh. (*anxiously*) I hope he'll be all right. He's so . . . sensitive.

Poopay He mentioned Rachel.

Ruella Rachel? Oh, she's Jessica's daughter. She's nineteen. Great strapping thing. At university in the States. We never see her.

Poopay Don't you get on?

Ruella She and I did, surprisingly. Briefly. For a time. But – she and Reece . . . She never really got over the death of her mother. Maybe she suspected something all along. Maybe. She and her mother were very close, apparently. Yes, that would explain a lot . . . (*She reflects.*)

Poopay (*thoughtfully*) What we need, really, of course, is that confession.

Ruella Confession?

Poopay The one that Reece wrote and signed. The one I witnessed.

Ruella Reece wrote a confession?

Poopay Yes, didn't I tell you? That's why I was there. Just to sign it. And he wanted me to deliver it for him.

Ruella Where to?

Poopay Chambers, Grady and suchlike . . .

Ruella That bunch of crooks? Don't tell me they're still going?

Poopay Apparently.

Ruella You see, there's no justice. Absolutely none. Well, splendid. We need this confession, don't we? Where is it now?

Poopay Stuffed down the bidet in his bathroom.

Ruella Oh yes? We'd better rescue it then, hadn't we?

Poopay I'm sorry, I'm not going back there. Not with that Julian –

Ruella We'll go together. We can tackle him together. The two of us.

Poopay Have you seen him lately?

Ruella Well, he must be – he must be getting on a bit. By then.

Poopay I'd hate to meet him in his prime, that's all I can say.

Ruella You might in a minute if we don't get a move on. All right. Through that door, get the confession, back here, regroup, through the door again, tackle Jessica, show her the confession, back here, regroup and get the hell out of here before Julian arrives. How does that sound?

Poopay Question. Why don't you just get the hell out of here? If you're not here, he can't kill you?

Ruella One, because my running away doesn't save an innocent woman from drowning, does it? Two, my running away won't improve your chances by much, I fancy. And three, I never, never, ever run away.

Poopay (*admiringly*) Reece said you were like that.

Ruella Like what?

Poopay Good. A good person.

Ruella (*rather embarrassed*) Oh, really? You should try playing bridge with me.

Poopay What if we can't get through? Say that door doesn't work any more?

Ruella Then we'll both stand on that window sill and wait for Julian. But we're not going to do that, are we? All right? Are you fit?

Poopay (*very reluctant*) Yes.

Ruella Who's going first?

Poopay You are. You're braver than me.

Ruella Don't believe it, I'm terrified. Right, go, go, go . . .

They move to the intercommunicating door. Ruella opens it. Poopay hangs back a little.

I think there's only room for one of us in here. As soon as I'm through, follow on. The layout's exactly the same as this, is it?

Poopay Exactly the same.

Ruella Yes. I think they may even all be the same room, you know. Wish me luck.

Poopay Yes.

Ruella closes the door. Poopay stands close to it on the other side, listening. Close enough so that when the unit revolves, as it now does, both women revolve with it. Poopay remains listening at the far door.

Ruella opens the near door. The room is in darkness for a minute. She edges in.

Before she can close the door, the bathroom lights come on. A shrill squeal and Jessica, wrapped only in her sheet, comes racing through the bathroom via the bedroom door. Reece is chasing her. His hair is soaking wet from an earlier dowsing. He has a glass of water in his hand and is attempting to catch Jessica and repay her.

Ruella (*realizing where she is*) Oh, no . . .

Before she can retreat, Jessica has raced through the bathroom and into the sitting room. Reece still in pursuit, switches on the sitting room lights. The couple stop dead as they see Ruella.

Jessica (*startled*) Oh!

Reece (*likewise*) Ah!

Ruella Look, I'm frightfully sorry –

Reece (*angrily*) Right. I am now getting the house detective.

Ruella Look, there's no need, there's absolutely no need, honestly. Wrong room again. I'm so sorry. (*Ruella gets back into the lobby and closes the door.*)

Jessica What does she want, Reece? Why does she keep breaking in here?

Reece (*striding to the bedroom*) Come on. I'm phoning the house detective . . .

Jessica (*following him*) Yes. But what did she want, Reece? Who is she?

The couple go into the bedroom. Ruella revolves in the unit once more. She opens the door and Poopay steps back.

Poopay I couldn't get in. You didn't close the other door. Well?

Ruella (*a little breathless*) Wrong place, wrong time, wrong people. I went back instead of forwards. I don't know how you control it. It may depend on who goes in first. You'd better try it.

Poopay Me?

Ruella Yes, go on. In you go. (*She bustles her in.*) I'll be right behind you. (*half to herself*) At least I hope I will. (*to Poopay*) If you finish up in the honeymooners' bedroom instead, you'd better beat it quick. They're getting rather shirty.

Poopay If I finish up there, I'm getting into bed with them, don't worry.

Ruella Good luck.

Ruella closes the door behind Poopay. The unit revolves, as before, this time with Ruella on the outside.
Poopay opens the far door. The lights, again, come on in the bathroom but this time it is Julian.
A groan from Reece in the bedroom.

Julian (*calling as he comes in*) . . . all right, all right. I'll get you a flannel. A cold flannel . . . (*He grabs a face flannel and runs it under the cold tap.*)

Poopay Oh, God. . . .

Reece (*off, weakly*) I need ice, Julian, I need some ice . . .

Julian (*calling*) You can't have ice, I've told you. You put ice on your head you'll freeze your brain. (*muttering to* *himself*) Bloody good idea, too, if you ask me . . . (*He goes back into the bedroom, killing the lights as he goes.*)

Poopay closes her door and revolves back. Ruella lets her out.

Poopay He's there! Julian. I saw him.

Ruella (*excitedly*) You got there?

Poopay He was in the bathroom. Getting Reece a flannel. He seems to be nursing him.

Ruella Yes. He would. I think Reece is probably the only person Julian really cares for . . .

Poopay And Reece? Is he fond of Julian?

Ruella (*tersely*) Reece cares for no one but Reece. Listen, Phoebe, I think I may have some rather bad news. I have a nasty feeling you're going to have to go in there on your own.

Poopay On my own?

Ruella I've been thinking about it. I don't think this thing allows us to travel forward. Only backwards.

Poopay What do you mean? I just travelled forwards.

Ruella Yes, you did. But you were going back to where you came from.

Poopay Forwards?

Ruella Right. Whereas I can only go back to Jessica and then forwards again to here.

Poopay (*just about comprehending*) Oh, yes. What about Jessica?

Ruella Jessica? She can't go anywhere. Well, she might be able to go even further back, but that's not a lot of use, is it?

Poopay She could strangle Julian at birth. Stop him murdering his mother, anyway.

Ruella The point is, I couldn't follow you just now. I tried. (*indicating the door, apologetically*) Sorry.

Poopay So I have to go, do I?

Ruella I'm afraid so. I tell you what, I'll do the Jessica trip. How about that? Anyway, I have a suspicion there may be a limit to the distance we can travel individually. Interesting. If we really wanted to go back a long way, say to Shakespearian times, for instance, we'd have to set up a sort of relay team, with different people handing over every twenty years. Wouldn't that be fascinating?

Poopay Yes, I can't wait. To be or not to be. Pass it on.

Ruella I'll be here. Promise. First sign of trouble, come straight back.

Poopay You're telling me that? (*She looks at the door and takes a deep breath.*) This is only because you lent me your coat and you haven't got long to live, I'm doing this. I wouldn't do this for everyone. (*She steps into the lobby.*) If I go missing . . . you travel straight back and stop me from doing this.

Ruella You'll come back. I know you will. Don't worry. Good luck.

Poopay Goodbye. (*muttering*) I'm mad. I'm mad doing this.

> *Ruella closes the door. She goes straight to her bedroom as Poopay revolves in the lobby. Poopay opens the far door. She is back in 2014, as before.*
> *The suite is in darkness, except for a light through the bedroom doorway. Julian appears to be reading to Reece, who groans now and then. Poopay listens,*

somewhat amazed, for a second then makes her way
cautiously to the bathroom.

Julian (*off, from the bedroom*) . . . 'Before I had time to
listen much for the approach of footsteps, Ruth came
back, and behind her Lorna; coy as if of her bridegroom;
and hanging back with her beauty. Ruth banged the door
and ran away; and Lorna stood before me –'

Reece groans. Poopay has reached the bathroom
doorway safely. She freezes.

I'm not reading much more of this, you know. Are you
going to sleep soon?

Reece (*weakly*) Go on, go on . . .

Julian (*reading*) 'But she did not stand for an instant,
when she saw what I was like. At the risk of all thick
bandages, and upsetting a dozen medicine bottles, and
scattering leeches right and left, she managed to get into
my arms, although they could not hold her. She laid her
panting warm young breast on the place where they meant
to bleed me, and she set my pale face up; and she would
not look at me, having greater faith in kissing.'

As Julian resumes reading, Poopay continues on her
way. She reaches the bidet and fumbles around to find
the hidden document. She accidentally turns on the tap.
A jet of water squirts into her face.

Poopay Shit!

She listens. Julian's voice drones on from the other
room. Poopay fumbles about some more and finds the
document.
Poopay, during the next, returns through the
bathroom door holding the document. She is more
confident now. Perhaps too confident.

Julian (*reading*) 'I felt my life come back, and glow; I felt my trust in God revive; I felt the joy of living and of loving dearer things than life. It is not a moment to describe; who feels can never tell of it. But the compassion of my sweetheart's tears, and the caressing of my bride's lips, and the throbbing of my wife's heart (now at last at home on mine) made me feel that the world was good, and not a thing to be weary of. Little more have I to tell' – thank God for that – 'The doc –'

At this point, Poopay falls over a piece of furniture, probably the same piece of furniture she fell over in Ruella's room. Julian stops reading.

What's that?

Poopay makes it to the intercommunicating door as Julian comes into the sitting room, still holding the book. He is in his shirt sleeves. Incongruously, he is wearing Poopay's discarded blonde wig. As he switches on the lights, Poopay just makes it into the lobby, closing the door behind her. She stands there while her nerves steady.

Reece (*off, feebly*) What was that, Julian? Who was that?

Julian (*as he straightens the furniture*) Nothing, Reece, old son. Just a rodent. Probably a rat.

Reece (*off*) Rats. Better put some poison down.

Julian I will, Reece, I will. Soon as I've got you to sleep.

Julian switches off the lights and goes back into the bedroom.
    Poopay revolves and returns to Ruella's room. She opens the door and comes out hurriedly.

Poopay (*excitedly*) I got it, I – (*looking round the empty room*) Ruella? Ruella? (*in panic*) Oh my God, I'm in the wrong room, I'm in the wrong room . . . (*loudly*) Ruella!

Ruella comes hurrying out of the bedroom. She has changed.

Ruella (*alarmed*) Phoebe!

Poopay Oh, thank God.

Ruella You all right?

Poopay Yes. I couldn't see you. I thought I was – I was . . .

Ruella You got it!

Poopay (*handing the document to her*) I got it.

Ruella Oh, well done. (*skimming through it*) Oh, this is marvellous. (*reading some more*) Oh, this is unbelievable. I don't know how they got away with half of this. Well, they're not going to, are they? I thought I'd better get dressed this time. If I was going back again. I think Jessica was beginning to suspect that Reece was seeing someone else on the side. Little does she know. He's barely got the energy for – (*looking at the document*) – yes, here it is. Listen. (*reading*) 'On 5 October 1994, my second wife Ruella met her death when apparently she fell from a sixth-floor window of her suite in the Regal Hotel' – God, it's eerie reading this – 'Let it be known that it was no accident. That my colleague Julian Goodman also confessed to me to her murder. Apparently, on the night in question he entered her bedroom while she was asleep and having knocked her unconscious, threw her from the window . . .' (*She stops reading and sways slightly, clearly distressed. Smiling weakly*) He's got the most appalling style, hasn't he? (*She sits.*)

Poopay You OK?

Ruella Yes. Felt a bit dizzy, that's all. I'll be fine.

Poopay (*grasping her shoulders*) Deep breaths. (*pressing her down*) Head between the knees . . .

Ruella (*complying*) Thank you. Yes. It's reading it – in his handwriting . . . Stupid . . .

Poopay Not stupid. God almighty, it's not stupid. Not at all.

Ruella straightens up.

Better?

Ruella Thank you. Well, at least we're certain it's tonight, at any rate. Better get our skates on. I'll tackle Jessica. You stay here. Lock that door. Put the chain on. Don't open it to anyone. If someone knocks, tell them they've got the wrong room. I'll be back as quick as I can.

Poopay I think I'd rather try and come with you.

Ruella I honestly don't think you should. (*gently*) I think this has got to be between me and Jessica. Just wives, you know. You understand?

Poopay (*a little hurt*) No. Right. I'll stay here, it's OK.

Ruella opens the intercommunicating door.

Ruella Have a shower, if you like. Or a bath. Help yourself to some proper clothes, you can't keep wandering round like that. There must be something of mine that would do you. See you in a minute.

Poopay See you.

Ruella And remember. Lock that door.

Poopay waves rather limply as Ruella shuts the door. She looks rather lonely and lost. She goes and locks the front door. She then goes into the bathroom and looks apprehensively at the shower.

63

Poopay (*to herself*) I'm not taking a shower. (*She goes into the bedroom.*)

Ruella revolves inside the unit. She opens the door. The room is silent and in complete darkness. She starts to creep across towards the bedroom. She is midway there when the room is flooded with light. Harold, a younger Harold aged thirty-five, who has been lurking in the shadows by the front doorway, stands triumphantly, his hand still on the light switch.

Harold (*in a triumphant whisper*) Gotcher!

Ruella Now, listen – I'm . . .

Before she can protest, Harold has grasped her by the arm and is propelling her to the door.

Harold (*still sotto*) Come on, you. Out. This is a private room.

Ruella I wish you'd let me explain –

Harold Sshhh!

Jessica comes out of the bedroom, now in her night clothes.

Jessica (*sotto*) Have you got her? Well done, well done, well done . . .

Harold Sorry to have disturbed you, madam, I –

Jessica Ssssh! My husband's asleep.

Harold Oh. (*quietly*) Sorry you've been disturbed, madam. I'll get her downstairs –

Ruella Harold, don't be so ridiculous, I need to speak to this woman . . .

Harold Harold? Oh, Harold, is it?

Jessica Do you know her?

Harold Never seen her before in my life.

Ruella Jessica!

Harold Hoy, Mrs Welles. This is Mrs Welles. And Mr Palmer to you, all right?

Ruella Listen, I really must talk to this woman –

Jessica Ssshh!

Harold Ssshh!

Ruella (*sotto, to Jessica*) You must let me talk to you, Jessica. It's vitally important.

Harold (*dragging her*) Come on, now. (*to Jessica*) We get them occasionally, you know. Trying to relive their honeymoons, you know.

Jessica Really?

Harold It happens. Especially middle-aged women. They get repressed. Want to relive it all, second hand.

Ruella Oh, do shut up, you stupid man –

Harold (*cautioning*) Hey! Hey! Hey!

Ruella – with your half-baked, flabby psychology . . . No woman in her right mind would want to relive her honeymoon –

Jessica (*sotto, furious*) Get her out! Just get her out of here –

Harold (*getting Ruella as far as the door*) I am getting her out –

Ruella (*one last attempt*) Jessica!

Jessica (*hissing at her*) Yes, what, what what?

65

Ruella (*holding out the confession*) Would you please just read this. Please.

Jessica What is it?

Ruella Please.

Jessica Is it dirty?

Ruella No. It's not dirty. But it is very, very important. It concerns your life. Please. Promise me. Take it somewhere quiet and read it.

Jessica You're quite, quite mad, you know. You're potty and absolutely batty. All right, give it here. You've ruined my wedding night. (*She takes it from Ruella.*)

Ruella (*relieved*) Thank you. Thank you. I'll be downstairs if you –

Harold No, you won't, you'll be out in the street –

He drags Ruella finally through the front door.

(*a parting shot to Jessica*) I wouldn't bother reading it, madam. It'll just be filth. Pure filth. (*He closes the door.*)

Jessica stands a little puzzled. She looks at the document, probably with no great intention of reading it. She is rapidly drawn in. She frowns and walks slowly into the bedroom. As she does so, the lights cross fade and we are back in Ruella's room.

Poopay comes out of the bedroom and into the bathroom. She has shed her costume and is now in a borrowed bathrobe. She is evidently about to have a bath. She turns on the taps and checks the temperature. To fill in the time she examines her face in the bathroom mirror.

In the sitting room, the unit slowly revolves. It contains Julian, now wigless but still in his shirt sleeves. He opens the door and steps into the room. He

66

looks around, a trifle surprised to see where he is. Hearing the sounds from the bathroom he moves over to the door. Poopay remains unaware of his presence. Julian carefully opens the door. He sees her and smiles. He closes the door. Poopay turns and sees him. She gives a stifled scream.

Julian (*smiling at her*) Well, this is nice. Is it bath time, then?

He begins to advance on her, rolling up his sleeves as he does so. Poopay backs away. Before Julian can reach her:

A fade to

BLACKOUT

Act Two

The same. A few minutes later.
  *Lights up on Reece and Jessica's suite. Jessica is
standing, still in her night attire, the confession in her
hand. Her husband, Reece, is in the bedroom asleep, as
presumably is 'old' Reece in his corresponding room.*
  *In Ruella's suite there is no sign of either Julian or
Poopay.*
  The doorbell in Jessica's suite chimes.

Jessica (*as of reflex*) Sshhh!

  *She goes to the door and opens it. Harold is there with
  Ruella.*

(*seeing them*) Sshhh! Come in. My husband's still asleep.

Harold (*softly*) I don't know why you want her back in
here, I really don't.

Jessica (*ignoring him, to Ruella*) Please sit down.

Ruella Thank you for seeing me. Thank you.

  *Jessica waves Ruella to the sofa. Jessica sits in the chair.
  Ruella sits on the sofa. Harold sits next to Ruella.*

Jessica (*waving the document*) I called you back up here
because I demand to know where you got this? Where? I
want to know.

Ruella It's a complicated story –

Jessica Did you write it?

Ruella No, of course I didn't. It's quite clearly Reece's –

my hus – your husband's writing. You can see that.

Jessica Nonsense.

Ruella It's his signature.

Jessica How can it possibly be?

Ruella Look at it. Just look at it, girl, it's Reece's signature.

Jessica (*scrutinizing it again*) Well – it's like it. A bit. It's dreadfully wobbly.

Ruella Well, it would be. He was very old and ill when he signed it.

Jessica (*squeaking indignantly*) What are you talking about?

Ruella I am trying to tell you that that document is a true confession by your husband. A confession he made just before he died, forty years from now and which he gave to a prostitute named Phoebe in the year 2014 who somehow managed to get it to me, Ruella Welles, his second wife in the year 1994 and I am now giving it to you, Jessica Welles, his first wife, in 1974. Is that clear enough for you?

Jessica and Harold stares at her. A silence.

Harold I warned you not to let her back in.

Ruella (*calmer*) It's very important you take that document seriously, Jessica.

Jessica You are mad, aren't you? You're really quite, quite loony. You're like those people who bang on doors with Bibles.

Harold Excuse me. May I enquire as to the nature of this document?

Jessica It's just a load of lies and a forgery. That's all it is.

Harold May I be allowed to see it?

Ruella It's not a forgery.

Harold May I see it?

Jessica hands him the document.

Thank you. (*holding it up to the light*) Soon tell if it's a forgery.

Ruella How on earth could you?

Harold There are ways.

Ruella How can you possibly tell? You've got nothing to compare it with, you fool. Oh, you're such a stupid man.

Harold Hey! Hey!

Jessica (*hissing*) Keep your voices down. My husband's asleep. (*by way of an afterthought*) Sshhh!

Ruella (*muttering*) Take more than this to wake him up.

Jessica (*suspiciously*) What?

Ruella Nothing.

Harold (*to Ruella*) Any more from you and it's the police, all right? You have been warned. (*turning to Jessica*) Now. Have you a specimen of your husband's handwriting?

Jessica No, I haven't.

Harold Got his signature anywhere around? (*He looks about him.*)

Jessica No, of course I haven't. He doesn't walk about writing his name on everything.

Harold Maybe you could wake him up.

Jessica (*very angrily*) I am not waking him up just to sign his name. That thing is obviously a forgery – it can't possibly be true – so what would be the point? (*to Ruella*) Now listen to me. I called you back here for one reason. I don't know what you want, what you're after –

Ruella I want to help you –

Jessica Let me finish. You've said all you're going to say, now I'm going to say something. I'm going to destroy this filth now –

Ruella makes to protest.

– now and forget all about it. But if you ever, ever circulate anything of this nature again, if you ever even so much as pester me or my husband again – well, my father is very wealthy and influential and –

Ruella I know he was. Why the hell do you think Reece married you?

Jessica (*tearfully*) You will not say that. You will never say things like that again. How dare you say that!

Ruella I'm sorry, that was thoughtless. I'm sorry. But you've read the thing. You can see what Reece is like. You can see what he turns into.

Jessica (*distraught, to Harold*) Tear that up, please! Tear that up, now!

Ruella No, you mustn't. It's the only evidence we have.

Harold (*who has been studying the document during this*) Might as well destroy it. It's definitely a forgery. Look – word spelt wrong here.

Ruella Well, Reece could never spell –

Jessica No, he can never sp – (*She breaks off and stares at Ruella for a second.*)

71

Harold Excuse my asking, in this document are you intended to be this Jessica?

Jessica What do you mean? I am Jessica.

Harold She's got that bit right, then.

Jessica That doesn't prove a thing. Our engagement was announced in every single newspaper.

Harold It says here you die in seven years' time. In 1981.

Jessica I know it does. It's all horrible.

Harold Broken any mirrors lately, have you? (*He laughs.*) Death threats as well, then. (*He looks at Ruella accusingly.*)

Ruella Death threats, don't be absurd. You don't make death threats like that: 'Give me the money or you will die in seven years . . .'

Harold Does that say that in here?

Ruella No, of course it doesn't . . .

Harold Because if it says that in here . . .

Jessica (*getting slightly irritated with Harold as well*) It doesn't.

Harold And who's this Julian man? The one who's supposed to be doing all this killing? Have you ever heard of him?

Jessica Yes. Julian Goodman. He's my husband's very oldest friend. He was best man at our wedding today – yesterday. God, look at the time. What are we doing? I have to get up in the morning.

Harold (*handing back the document to Jessica*) Quite. We all have. Heard enough, have you?

Jessica Quite enough.

Harold (*to Ruella*) Come on, then.

Ruella Jessica . . . this is my final appeal. Please, please, please do not ignore or destroy that document. I beg you. Your life is in danger. So is mine. So is – so are a number of other people's.

Jessica (*affected by her tone, gently as if to a child*) Look. I don't think you actually mean any harm, do you? I really don't. I just think you're a bit – well – funny in the head. But you must stop this now. You mustn't do this sort of thing. Don't you see it upsets people? It makes me very upset when you write nasty things about my husband. Can't you see that? I mean – I mean, I don't know if you even have one – but imagine someone writing things like that about your husband. Can you imagine what it would be like?

Ruella That is my husband –

Jessica (*continuing gently*) No, he's not, you see. He's not your husband, he's my husband. Now, if you want a husband you're going to have to find one of your own.

Ruella Dear God, you're a stupid girl, aren't you? No wonder he drowned you.

Harold Now! That's enough of that. This lady is being extremely patient with you. Personally, I'd have chucked you out of that window, ten minutes ago.

Ruella Save someone else the job, anyway –

Jessica (*still reasonable*) Even if we accepted that this – nonsense – was true, you then want us to believe that you've somehow travelled back from 19 – whenever . . .

Ruella I'm not pretending it's easy to accept. It happens to be the fact.

Harold How did you get here, then? Where did you park your machine?

Ruella I came through that cupboard –

Harold Oh, you parked it in the cupboard, did you? That's a good idea. Very handy. Won't get a ticket in there, will you – ?

Ruella Would you shut up!

Jessica Sshhh!

Harold (*to Ruella*) Right, that is it. It's the police for you. We go downstairs and I am phoning the police. Breaking and entering. Three times. Demanding money with menaces. Slander. Libel –

Ruella (*savagely*) What about punching a house detective on the nose?

Jessica crosses to the intercommunicating door.

Jessica (*calming them*) Now, now, now, now! (*still infuriatingly reasonable*) Look. (*She opens the door.*) There's no machine in here, is there? Look for yourself. Can you see a machine? I can't.

Harold That door should be locked.

Ruella You can't see a machine because there isn't a machine.

Harold You just said there was a machine.

Ruella I did not. You said there was a machine. I never mentioned a machine.

Harold You've got to have a machine. You can't travel without a machine –

Jessica (*loudly*) You can't travel *with* a machine, either. What are you both talking about?

Ruella⎫
Harold⎭ Sshhh!

Jessica Sorry.

Ruella (*calmer*) There is no machine. You just step in there and close the door and – you travel. In time. You come out of the other door and there's – this same room – in a different time. If I stepped in there now, when I opened the other door I'd be in 1994. In 1994 I'm actually staying in this very room. This is my room then, you see.

Harold I doubt it. They're not going to let you back in here in a hurry.

Ruella glares at him.

Ruella I'm not going to forget this. I meet you much later, you know.

Harold Oh no, you don't. And I tell you for why. In 1994, you're not going to find me still here. Even if they did let you in. Oh, no. Because you know where I'll be? Cruising the Med. Cruising. In my own boat. 42 foot. Twin screw. Flying bridge. The Med. All right? That's where I'll be.

Ruella Want to bet?

Harold That's the plan.

Jessica Listen. I just want to try and get through to this person – (*to Ruella*) If this cupboard does what you say it does, tell you what, why don't we all have a travel together?

Ruella We can't. It only works for me.

Harold Ah, now it only works for her.

Jessica Why won't it work for us?

75

Harold You'll never convince her –

Ruella Well, it might work for you. But it probably wouldn't take you to the same place that I'd go. You'd go backwards not forwards, you see.

Harold (*laughing*) Dear, oh dear, oh dear. It gets worse, doesn't it? Go anywhere near Clapham, does it? You can drop me off on the way.

Ruella God knows where he'd go –

Harold I tell you exactly where I'd go. Where we'd all go, for that matter. Through that communicating door, straight through to a second communicating door – which should also be locked, incidentally – straight through that into a small utility room which in turn leads out via another door which should definitely be kept locked at all times, where we'd find ourselves in that hallway there. All right?

Ruella No, we wouldn't.

Harold Are you trying to teach me about my own hotel?

Jessica Oh come on, for goodness sake. Let's go and look. Get it over and done with. We're flying to Jamaica at 10.30. (*She moves back to the communicating door.*)

Harold Just a minute. If we're going, we're all going together.

Ruella We can't. We can't all get in at once.

Jessica All right then, I'll go first.

Harold No, no, no. I'm not having you going in there on your own.

Jessica Oh, don't be so silly.

Harold She could have an accomplice.

Ruella I'd rather you didn't. If it did work for you, it might complicate things no end.

Harold (*to Ruella*) Well, *you're* not going in there on your own – I'm not that stupid.

Ruella laughs.

Jessica Then you'd better go in, hadn't you?

Harold Me?

Jessica Well, you won't let anybody else go.

Harold Who's going to keep an eye on her?

Jessica I will. She's perfectly harmless.

Harold Don't you believe it.

Jessica Go on.

Harold All right. I have my keys. I shall do the round trip in order to show you. (*indicating the front door*) I'll knock on that door. You let me in.

Jessica OK.

Harold Don't let her out of your sight. See you in about half a minute.

Harold steps through the door and closes it behind him. He opens the other door. The unit does not revolve, so he goes off.

Jessica (*as soon as he's gone*) Listen. Quickly. I'm going to let you go. He's talking of handing you over to the police and even though you're utterly mad, you don't deserve that. I'm keeping this document and I'm going to destroy it. All I ask in return is your solemn promise that you won't do this again. Do you promise?

Ruella (*wearily*) Oh, dear heaven . . .

*Jessica puts the document in the pocket of her
bathrobe.*

Jessica If you can, try and see a doctor. Ask if he can
recommend someone to help you . . . Promise me?

Ruella (*giving up*) I don't know what else I can do. All
right. Promise.

Jessica Good. Good. That's a start. (*moving to the front
door*) Now, come on quickly. He'll be round in a minute.

Ruella (*a last sudden, desperate idea*) Jessica!

Jessica What?

Ruella Give me a piece of paper. Writing paper, quickly.

Jessica You're not going to write more of this stuff, are
you?

Ruella No. Please. Please.

Jessica I mean, you've just this second promised. Oh, all
right. (*crossing to the sideboard*) There should be some in
the drawer here somewhere.

Ruella And an envelope.

*Jessica finds some sheets of hotel notepaper and an
envelope in the drawer.*

Jessica Hotel paper, all right?

Ruella That'll do. Thank you. (*Ruella grabs the hotel pen
from the phone table and starts to scribble furiously.*)

Jessica He'll be back any second –

Ruella (*as she writes*) There's nothing I can say that will
convince you now – but – possibly – this might . . . (*She
finishes.*) There! (*She folds the paper and crams it into the
envelope.*)

There is a soft knock on the front door.

Jessica He's back.

Ruella (*sticking up the envelope*) I hope you'll be able to read it. It'd be absolutely ironic if you couldn't read it after all this.

Another, slightly louder knock on the door.

Jessica Do hurry up. I have to let him in.

Ruella (*scrawling something on the envelope*) Wait. There we are . . .

She gives the envelope to Jessica.

(*swiftly*) Please remember everything I've told you, terrible though it sounds. Keep that safely. Don't lose it. Please read it. Goodbye. God bless you. Have a nice honeymoon.

Ruella hugs Jessica briefly and kisses her on the forehead. Jessica is too startled to react. The door chime sounds.
   Ruella dashes to the communicating door, gives Jessica one last smile, goes inside and shuts herself in.
   As she does this, there is the sound of Harold's pass key in the front door. He enters just as Ruella closes her door.

Harold (*looking round the room*) Where is she?

Jessica (*vaguely*) She –

Harold (*indicating the communicating door*) She go through there?

Jessica (*lamely*) Yes.

Harold I asked you to keep an eye on her. I'll head her off.

Harold goes out, closing the front door. Jessica studies the envelope in her hand for the first time.

Jessica (*reading*) 'Not to be opened till 22 March 1975. Urgent and personal.' (*She shrugs.*) Mad. Utterly mad.

Reece (*off, from the bedroom, sleepily*) Jess! What's going on, Jess?

Jessica Nothing, darling, nothing. Go back to sleep . . .

> *Jessica goes into the bedroom, switching off the sitting room lights as she does so.*
>   *Simultaneously, Ruella revolves in the unit. She returns to her own room which is in darkness. She opens the door. When she finds the room without light she becomes instantly wary.*

Ruella (*softly*) Phoebe! Phoebe! (*a little louder*) Phoebe! (*to herself*) Oh, no.

> *She creeps across the darkened room. She reaches the bathroom door which is closed. She tries the handle and pushes gently on the door. It appears to be locked. Ruella pushes harder.*

(*starting to panic, getting louder*) Phoebe! Phoebe! No! No! (*beating on the door with her fists*) PHOEBE! Are you in there? Speak to me?

> *Poopay comes out of the bedroom. She is pale, shaken but unhurt. She appears to have been crying. She has exchanged her outfit for one belonging to Ruella. It sits uneasily on her. When she speaks she is very muted. She switches on the sitting room lights.*

Poopay Hallo . . .

Ruella (*startled*) Wah! Are you all right?

> *Poopay smiles blankly, still in shock. Ruella prattles on oblivious.*

Well, I saw Jessica. Showed her the confession. Tried to

explain. Left her a note she was to read later. I don't think she was terribly convinced, though. Actually, she's really awfully dim . . . That's nice that dress on you. Suits you. I suppose you find it a bit old fashioned. (*Another slight pause.*) Well, come on. No time to lose. Let's get out of here and check in somewhere else. Before Julian arrives. If he's coming. I'll just get my bag and a coat.

Poopay He's been.

Ruella What?

Poopay Julian's been. He was here.

Ruella (*horrified*) Julian was *here*?

Poopay nods.

Where were you? I mean –

Poopay (*in a whisper*) In the bathroom.

Ruella What happened?

Poopay (*starting to go to pieces*) He tried to drown me . . .

Ruella (*holding her*) Drown you?

Poopay (*speaking between sobs*) . . . he ran the bath . . . and then he held me under the water . . .

Ruella Under the water?

Poopay . . . yes . . .

Ruella Dear heaven.

Ruella draws Poopay down on to the sofa, and continues to comfort her.

Poopay (*muffled*) . . . I couldn't breathe . . . I was choking . . .

Ruella Then how did you – ? How did you get away?

Poopay . . . fell over . . .

Ruella Fell over? Who fell over?

Poopay . . . he fell over . . .

Ruella Julian fell over? What made him fall over?

Poopay He stood on the soap . . .

Ruella The soap?

Poopay Banged his head on the toilet.

Ruella Is he dead?

Poopay I don't know.

Ruella Is he still in there?

Poopay No.

Ruella Well, where is he?

Poopay He's in here.

Ruella (*very alarmed*) In here? Where in here?

Poopay We're sitting on him.

Ruella (*leaping up*) My God!

Poopay also gets up and points rather ineffectually at the sofa. She is still very distraught.

Poopay He's under there . . .

Ruella How did he get under there, for heaven's sake?

Poopay . . . I dragged him out here . . . and then I pulled the sofa over him to stop him getting up again . . .

Ruella Well, that's practical, anyway. How long's he been under there . . . ?

Poopay Ages.

Ruella I'd better take a look. (*moving back to the sofa, cautiously*) Which end is his head? Can you remember?

Poopay (*pointing*) That end.

Ruella Right. (*Ruella lifts the skirt off the sofa, carefully.*)

Poopay (*tearfully*) Don't let him out!

Ruella I'm not going to let him out, for goodness sake. I just want to see if he's alive. Though I should imagine if the lavatory didn't get him, then this sofa certainly has. (*Ruella bends to examine the unseen figure as best she can.*) Well, I'm no doctor but I have to say he looks pretty damn dead to me. Well done.

Poopay (*starting to cry again*) I'm a murderer now.

Ruella A murderer? A *murderer*? The man came into your bedroom, tried to drown you and slipped on a bar of soap. How does that make you a murderer?

Poopay They won't believe me. They'll never believe me.

Ruella You won't be here. You can go back now. You're safe. He's dead. He can't hurt you any more. Think of that.

Poopay (*a trifle calmer*) Yes.

Ruella Now come on, cheer up, Phoebe. The worst is over. You're safe. Say it. I'm safe now.

Poopay (*nearly convinced*) I'm safe now.

At this moment, Julian's bare arm shoots out through the base of the sofa, between the cushions, as in a spasm. Both women scream and rush to different corners of the room. The hand rises, the fist clenches and unclenches. The arm goes limp and flops back.

Ruella and Poopay watch horrified. A silence.

Ruella (*nervously*) It's just migor rortis, that's all it is . . .

Poopay What?

Ruella Rigor – mortis.

Poopay Yes. (*slight pause*) How do you know it's rigor mortis?

Ruella I don't. I'm guessing. He can't possibly be alive, though. He's been lying there with half a ton of horsehair on his face. He must be dead. We're all right. We're safe. Keep saying it. We're safe.

Poopay I may be safe. What about you? How are you going to explain him? He didn't try to drown you, did he?

Ruella They're not to know that.

Poopay They might want to know how he's suddenly aged twenty years overnight, though.

Silence.

Ruella That is a very, very good point. (*She ponders.*) And it's my problem. It's not yours. Off you go. Leave it to me. Back to your own time.

Poopay No.

Ruella Why not? What's to keep you?

Poopay Because I never, never, ever run away.

Ruella looks at her and smiles. Poopay nods.

Ruella No, what we need is help. Help to dispose of the body elsewhere. But who? Who?

Poopay I don't know anyone. Not here. I know a few back home could do it.

Ruella Yes, of course. I do know someone. The very man. (*with sudden decisiveness*) Yes! (*Ruella goes to the phone and punches 0.*)

Poopay Who are you calling?

Ruella puts her finger to her lips to silence Poopay.

Ruella Hallo . . . I wonder if you could tell me – is Mr Palmer of security still on duty . . .? Oh, splendid. I wonder if you'd mind paging him for me? It's Mrs Welles in suite 647 . . . Thank you so much . . . (*She waits.*)

Poopay Security? You're not getting bloody security up here?

Ruella Not any bloody security. This one owes me. (*into phone*) Hallo . . . Mr Palmer – Harold. It's Mrs Welles. Suite 647, yes. Mr Palmer, we have a most delicate problem up here . . . that does require the utmost tact . . . I wonder if you could possibly help us? I would be most terribly grateful . . . Yes . . . Oh, would you? . . . thank you . . . That would be most kind . . . Bye. (*She rings off.*) Appalling man. Right. Action. He'll be three minutes. Take that end. (*She moves to one end of the sofa and grasps the arm.*)

Poopay What are you doing? What do you think you're doing?

Ruella Explain as we go. Come along, give me a hand. We have to move this off him.

Poopay I'm not moving that. He's staying under there.

Ruella If he stays under here, we can hardly pass it off as an accident, can we? Not even Harold Palmer's going to believe that the man just crawled under the sofa to die. Now do help, Phoebe. Trust me.

Poopay (*taking the other end of the sofa*) If he moves, I'm out of here, I tell you.

85

Ruella If he moves, I'm right behind you.

Together they manoeuvre the sofa off Julian.

Right. Whew. How on earth did you move this thing on your own?

Poopay Raw naked panic.

Ruella kneels to examine Julian.

Careful!

Ruella It's all right, he really is very, very dead. Could hardly be deader. (*dropping his arm*) Look at that . . .

Poopay (*averting her gaze*) Ugggh!

Ruella (*who seems to be enjoying herself*) Yes, good. No surface bleeding. All internal. Ought to fool Harold, anyway. Now, we have to drag him into the bedroom. Phoebe . . .

Poopay (*backing away*) I can't. I can't touch him.

Ruella looks at her. Poopay stands there.

Ruella (*deliberately*) Phoebe! Phoebe, you're pathetic. You're just a feeble, snivelling little creature . . .

Poopay (*rallying*) Don't call me that. You haven't –

Ruella What else are you, then? What else are you?

Poopay (*angrily*) It's all right for you, you haven't been nearly bloody drowned, have you?

Ruella It's a pity he didn't make a better job of it. You little wimp!

Poopay (*very angry*) You are asking for it, you know. You are really asking for it . . . you are going to get it in a minute, I don't care who you are . . . I've put people in hospital, you know, for that . . . You take that back. Nobody calls me that . . .

Ruella Right, I take it back. But you give me a hand. If you've any strength at all.

Poopay grabs Julian's arm and starts to drag the body across the floor single-handed.

Poopay (*aggressively*) I've got strength. Don't you worry. We'll soon see who's not got strength . . .

Ruella (*alarmed*) Careful! Don't damage him . . . Here!

They drag the body together towards the bedroom door.

He's a weight. Always looks so easy . . .

They pause momentarily for breath.

Poopay You did that deliberately, didn't you? Got me angry?

Ruella Come on. Pull.

Poopay Right. Don't ever call me that again, though. I'm not a prude but I can't stand that word.

They drag the body the rest of the way into the bedroom.

Ruella (*as they go*) What, wimp, you mean?

Poopay (*off*) Don't keep saying it!

Ruella (*off*) Why not? It only means ineffectual. Useless. That's all.

Poopay (*off*) Not where I come from, it doesn't.

Ruella (*off*) What does it mean where you come from?

Poopay (*off*) Never mind. Never you mind. I'm not repeating it.

Ruella (*off*) OK? One, two, three . . .

Both (*off*) Hup!

Ruella (*off, breathless*) Now we have to undress him and get him into bed . . .

Poopay (*off*) Oh, no . . .

Ruella (*off*) Phoebe . . .

Poopay (*off, hastily*) All right, all right, I know. Wimp! Wimp! Wimp! We're not getting in with him, are we?

Ruella (*off, disgusted*) Oh, Phoebe!

Poopay (*off*) Sorry.

The doorbell rings.

Ruella (*off*) That'll be Harold. You'll have to do that on your own.

Poopay (*off*) What? Undress him?

Ruella (*off*) Yes.

Poopay (*off*) Completely?

Ruella comes out of the bedroom. She straightens the sofa as best she can.

Ruella Of course completely. Come on, you've done it before, surely?

Poopay (*off*) Yes, but they're not usually dead, are they? (*a thought*) Oh, I don't know, though.

Ruella I'll keep him talking in here. Come out as soon as you've finished.

The doorbell chimes again. Ruella closes the bedroom door and goes and opens the front door. She admits the older Harold, fifty-five years old and far more deferential.

(*her totally charming self*) Harold, thank you so much for coming up. I know you must be terribly busy.

Harold Well, you know, crime marches on. (*He laughs.*) Now, what can I do for you? Something I can sort out? A small problem, is there?

Ruella No, it's quite a big problem actually, Harold. It's going to need your utmost discretion –

Harold I think we've got to know each other sufficiently over the years . . .

Ruella Oh, yes . . .

Harold . . . for you to feel that there's nothing I wouldn't do for you or for Mr Welles.

Ruella Yes, I'm sure. Though in this case, Mr Welles has to be kept out of it, I'm afraid.

Harold He does?

Ruella Yes, it's not something – he'd altogether approve of – if you follow me?

Harold looks puzzled. Ruella waits.

It's a matter of great delicacy – if you see what I mean, Harold . . .

Harold Delicacy? (*cottoning on*) Ah, I see what you mean. Delicacy.

Ruella Yes.

Harold Oh dear.

Poopay comes out of the bedroom. She nods to Ruella. Harold is aware of her and turns.

(*disapprovingly*) Evening.

Poopay Evening.

Ruella Harold, you remember –

Harold I remember. Phoebe, yes. (*He laughs and shakes his head.*)

   Poopay looks at him nastily.

You're still here, are you?

Poopay (*a nasty smile*) Yes.

Harold (*to Ruella*) Well, she looks a bit better. A shade of an improvement, anyway. (*confidentially, to Ruella*) She in on this, is she? Safe to talk in front of her? Or you want me to sling her out again?

Ruella No, no. I'm afraid Phoebe's very much in on this, as well. Very much so. Both of us . . .

Harold Oh. I see. I see. It was both of you, was it?

Ruella Yes.

Harold (*digesting this*) I see. (*awkwardly*) Are we talking – I take it we are talking about some form of Lesbianic relationship.

Ruella Good heavens, no!

Harold Oh, I'm sorry. I'm very sorry.

Ruella If we were up to that, Harold, we would hardly have sent for you, would we?

Harold (*confused*) – Er no, I suppose not.

Ruella We'd have been in there getting on with it, surely?

Harold (*embarrassed*) Yes, yes, presumably. I do beg your pardon if I've embarrassed you in any way.

Ruella No, our problem, Harold, is what to do with *him*.

Harold Him?

Ruella The man.

Harold Man? There's a man involved as well?

Ruella Obviously there's a man. We had to have a man, didn't we?

Harold We?

Ruella She and I.

Harold You and her?

Ruella Yes.

Harold You and her were in that bedroom with a man.

Ruella Yes.

Harold I see.

Ruella Come on, Harold, you've heard of threesomes, surely. This hotel must be bristling with them.

Harold Possibly. I've never had personal experience of them. Till now. (*He glares at Poopay.*) So? Where is the gentleman? Has he left?

Ruella No he's in there.

Harold I see, what is he, asleep in bed?

Ruella Not exactly.

Poopay He's dead.

Harold Dead?

Ruella Yes.

Harold Dead in that bed?

Ruella I'm afraid so. He collapsed, quite suddenly. I think both of us were just too much for him, don't you?

Poopay Yes. He bit off more than he could chew.

Harold (*coldly, to her*) That's a very distasteful image, if I may say so . . . (*to Ruella*) Well, you certainly have a problem here, Mrs Welles.

Ruella It gets worse, I'm afraid.

Harold Worse? You mean there were more persons involved?

Ruella No, you see – The man concerned also happens to be my husband's partner and best friend. It's Julian Goodman.

Harold Mr Goodman? It's Mr Goodman in there?

Ruella Yes. Do you remember him, Harold?

Harold I certainly do, yes. I know – knew Mr Goodman very well. Your husband's business associate. He often stays here.

Ruella He did.

Harold And he's the one who's dead in there?

Ruella I'm afraid so.

Harold Worse and worse.

Ruella Yes.

Harold Er, it's not my business but – from my impression of Mr Goodman, I would never have imagined that this was his sort of thing at all. He seemed more – well, up the other side of the ladder, if you follow me . . .

Ruella I think he just wanted to give it a try, you know.

Harold Yes. Went out with a bang then, didn't he?

Poopay That's a very distasteful way of putting it, if you don't mind my saying so.

Harold I'm sorry, Mrs Welles, I do appreciate your predicament, believe me, but I don't think I can possibly help you here. This involves a death, you understand. There's no way I can cover up a death. No way.

Ruella No, I'm not suggesting you should. Never for a minute. What I was hoping you might do is to help us alter the circumstances of the death.

Harold I don't quite follow.

Ruella Well, Mr Goodman died as a result of – over-exertion. Almost certainly a heart attack – anyway, natural causes – I think we can assume that, don't you?

Harold (*cautiously*) Yes . . .

Ruella Now, it is very possible that Mr Goodman could have had that same heart attack in a room on his own – while, say, moving his bed . . .

Harold (*dubious*) Moving his bed?

Ruella Or something equally solitary and strenuous. All I'm asking is that you help us move him to an empty room and maybe make a few minor alterations to the hotel register . . . That way, Mr Goodman can be discovered tomorrow morning, alone in bed, and without the least hint of scandal surrounding his death.

Harold Oh, I don't think I can do that. (*Pause.*) No, I don't think I can possibly agree to that. I'm sorry.

Ruella (*sighing*) Very well.

Harold I'm sorry. I mean normally, Mrs Welles, as I say . . .

Ruella I could – I know it's very wrong of me to say this, Harold – I could make this really worth your while . . .

Harold I don't think I can accept money –

Ruella Of course not. I wasn't thinking of money . . .

Harold (*rather disappointed*) Weren't you?

Ruella Kind. I was thinking more in kind, Harold.

Harold Kind? (*He looks at both the women.*) You mean – ? I don't know that that's quite my thing, actually.

Ruella No, no, no.

Poopay (*emphatically*) No.

Ruella I was thinking more – Well, you've been here what – ? Ages, haven't you?

Harold Since 1967 – 27 years . . .

Ruella But I'm sure you never planned to be here that long, did you?

Harold Well – no, if you must know, at one time I did have dreams. Don't we all?

Ruella You're still young enough to realize those dreams, Harold. Surely?

Harold Young enough, yes. But where's the money when you need it? I mean, it's not that I haven't saved – but the value of money, as such . . . plummeted through the floor, hasn't it?

Ruella Sad. So they all go out of the window, these dreams, do they? Cruising the Med, say. In your very own boat . . . twin screw . . .

Harold (*looking at her in amazement*) Flying bridge?

Ruella 42 foot . . .

Harold 50.

Ruella 44.

Harold 46.

94

Ruella Done.

Harold There's an empty suite on the third floor. We can take him in there.

Ruella Thank you, Harold.

Harold (*moving to the door*) I'll get a laundry skip from next door. (*Harold opens the front door.*) How did you know that? I never told anyone about that.

Ruella I suppose you must have done, at some stage. You've just forgotten.

Harold (*puzzled*) Yes. There was something I remembered, just now. Years ago. Some woman, she . . . Can't remember the details. (*starting to leave*) Let me in again. (*Harold goes out.*)

Poopay I'd hate to do business with you.

Ruella I think that's sorted that out.

Poopay I'll help him with the move. Don't you.

Ruella Are you sure?

Poopay Someone may see us. Look a bit odd if you were . . .

Ruella Yes, possibly.

Poopay I was just thinking about Jessica. Do you think she still died? Even after your note?

Ruella I think we have to assume she has. Sadly. We should have asked Harold. Maybe he knows what happened to her?

Poopay I think I'd sooner not know, in some ways . . .

The doorbell chimes. Poopay admits Harold. He pushes a large skip. Inside he has a sack full of clothing.

Harold Got it.

Ruella Well done.

Harold Had an inspiration, too. (*He holds up the sack.*) The sixth floor lost property bag. Clothing, various items, female. Strew some around down there. Make it look as if he had a woman in. He died, she scarpered. More convincing.

Harold pushes the skip into the bedroom. Poopay helps him guide it through the doorway.

Ruella Brilliant. Harold, you're brilliant.

Harold (*as he goes*) Amazing what they leave behind. Found a duck once, you know. In the bath. A live duck . . .

Ruella takes the opportunity to go into the bathroom and tidy away any evidence.

(*off, in the bedroom*) Better take his clothes as well.

Poopay (*off*) OK.

Harold (*off*) My God, what have you done to him? He's aged about twenty years.

Poopay (*off*) Yes, well, we gave him a good going over . . .

Harold (*off, incredulously*) Going over! You've destroyed his whole metabolism. Look at him. His hair's gone white. I don't know what it is you're into, girl, but don't invite me along.

Poopay (*off*) No problem.

Harold (*off*) Here we go then. Heave.

Sound of them lifting him into the skip.

Poopay (*off*) He won't fit in. He's too long.

Harold (*off*) Yes, he's a big lad. Here, use the sheet. Cover him with that.

Ruella (*calling*) You need a hand?

Harold (*off, calling*) No, we're all right. Everything under control.

Harold and Poopay come out of the bedroom as before, although this time the skip is loaded with Julian's body. This is mostly covered with the sheet except for the feet which stick out prominently. Ruella comes hurrying out of the bathroom as she hears them.

(*directing Poopay*) Mind the door, that's it . . . Keep going.

Ruella I'll hold the front door for you.

Harold Check the coast first.

Ruella Right. (*She opens the front door and looks both ways down the hall.*)

Harold (*to Poopay, impatiently*) Cover his feet. Cover up his feet then.

Poopay does so.

Ruella (*coming back in*) All clear.

Harold All right. (*to Poopay*) Go to the left. We'll use the service lift. Let's hope we make it.

Harold and Poopay start out of the front door. Ruella holds the door for them.

Ruella Got the room key?

Harold Got my master key. Opens everything. Won't be long.

Ruella Good luck. (*She closes the door behind them. She*

*stands for a second, surveying the room. She smiles to
herself. It has been a job well done. Yawning)* If I don't go
to bed in a minute, I'll die.

> *Ruella goes into her bedroom. Both the sitting room
> and the bathroom go to darkness.*
> *Immediately, there is the sound of the key in the lock
> and Harold and Poopay enter the third-floor suite with
> the skip. Harold switches on the lights.*

Harold Yes, here we are. 347. Empty suite. This'll do.
Bedroom's through there.

> *The two of them steer the skip to the bedroom.*

(directing Poopay) Mind the door, that's it . . . Keep
going.

> *The two of them go into the bedroom with the skip.*

(off) Right. Ready?

Poopay *(off)* Yeah.

Harold *(off)* And two-three hup!

Poopay *(off)* Huf!

Harold *(off)* That's it. Now, you have a look through that
lot. Sort out some suitable items of clothing to strew
around. I'll try and arrange things to look convincing in
here. Make it look like strenuous . . .

Poopay *(off)* Right.

Harold *(off)* Make sure they're suitable garments . . .

> *Poopay comes out of the bedroom with the bag of
> clothes.*

Poopay All right, I'm not stupid, you know . . .

Harold *(off)* Fooled me . . .

Poopay pulls a face at Harold through the door. She puts the bag on the sofa and starts to sort through it.

Poopay (*under her breath*) Wimp! (*calling to Harold as she does this*) Mrs Welles' husband . . .

Harold (*off*) Mr Reece Welles? What about him?

Poopay (*calling*) Did you ever know his first wife?

Harold (*off*) I did. Very charming young woman. Jessica. Well connected. Came from a very good family.

Poopay (*calling*) What happened to her? Do you know?

Harold (*off*) No idea. No concern of mine.

Poopay (*as casually as she can manage, calling*) Did they divorce or – did she die . . . or something?

Harold (*off*) I have not the faintest idea. If you're that interested, I should ask your close friend, Mrs Welles the second.

Poopay She doesn't know either.

Harold (*off*) What?

Poopay (*calling*) Nothing.

Harold (*off*) Just get on sorting those clothes.

Poopay (*calling*) I am. (*She finds an outfit she rather fancies – perhaps a smart, casual all-in-one outfit of some kind. More to herself*) This is nice. Haven't seen one of these for ages.

She looks towards the bedroom door to ensure Harold is still occupied. She swiftly starts to remove Ruella's dress and to change into the outfit.

What the hell? Lost property, isn't it?

As she does this, Ruella comes from the bedroom into

99

her bathroom, switching on the light as she does so. She has changed back to her bathrobe. She brings through her handbag and places it on the stool. At the wash basin, she starts preparing for bed.

At this stage, both women, Ruella and Poopay, begin to pursue the same chain of thought. Both are very tired, especially Ruella, so the process takes a little longer than usual. Thus as Poopay speaks it, Ruella thinks it.

(*to herself, as she changes*) . . . what I don't really understand is . . . if Julian's dead . . . then he can't possibly have killed Jessica . . . because he's dead. But then he's only dead . . . hang on . . . he's only dead in my time . . . even though he died in this time. Does that mean he's dead in this time just because he died in this time? Because if that's the case, then Jessica who's dead in our time, should be dead in her time. But she wasn't, she was alive. Before she died. Similarly Ruella, who's dead in my time, is still alive in this time. So if that's the case . . . even though Julian's dead in my time . . . he must in this time be . . . still . . . alive. (*yelling*) OH MY GOD, HE'S STILL ALIVE!

Ruella (*freezing in the middle of her tasks*) Of course! He's still alive!

Poopay rushes to the front door.
Harold comes dashing out of the bedroom.
Ruella runs back into the bedroom.

Harold Who's still alive?

Poopay Julian! He's still alive, I've got to warn her . . . Ruella! (*She runs out of the suite. The door closes behind her.*)

Harold Where are you going? (*He gathers up the bag of clothes, including Poopay's discarded Ruella dress.*) I don't know. (*realizing*) Still alive? He's still alive? Oh good grief!

I've just tied him to the bed rail! (*Harold hurries back into the bedroom.*)

Ruella simultaneously comes out of the bedroom back into the bathroom, struggling into her dress.

Ruella (*angrily, at herself*) Of course he's still alive, you stupid, damn woman! Think! You don't think, do you? (*She grabs up her handbag.*) Get out of here. Anywhere's got to be safer than here . . .

Ruella hurries to the front door and opens it. In the doorway is Julian, large as life and twenty years younger than we've ever seen him before.

Julian (*smiling*) Ruella . . . You're still awake . . .

Ruella (*stepping back, instinctively*) Julian –

Julian (*closing the door behind him*) Sorry to trouble you, I wondered if I could just have a quiet word?

Ruella (*standing her ground*) I'm sorry, I'm just on my way out.

Julian It's two in the morning, you can't be going out now, surely? You ought to be tucked up in bed.

Ruella If it's two in the morning what are you doing here?

Julian Just a quiet word, if I could?

Ruella (*louder*) Will you kindly get out of my way, please? I've told you, I'm going out.

Julian A very quiet word . . . (*He switches off the sitting room lights.*)

Ruella (*louder still*) What are you doing, Julian? How dare you? For the last time, get out of my way . . .

She tries to push past Julian. He is too quick for her.

One hand goes over her mouth, the other round her waist, trapping her arms to her sides. He starts to walk her towards the bedroom door.

Julian (*softly*) Now, I did say a quiet word, didn't I? Quietly now, please. Quietly. All right? That's it.

They go into the bedroom. A few vain gurgling noises from Ruella as they do so.
  The lights snap up as we return to the other suite. Harold comes into the bathroom with a handful of women's underwear. The doorbell chimes urgently several times.

Harold (*cautiously, calling from the doorway to sitting room*) Who is it?

Poopay (*off, outside*) Poopay! It's Poopay!

Harold (*baffled*) Poopay? Who the hell's Poopay?

Poopay (*off*) Phoebe! Let me in, Harold!

Harold opens the front door and admits Poopay.

Harold Where have you been? What do you want? You'll wake up everyone at this rate.

Poopay What's her number? I've forgotten the number of her suite.

Harold Who?

Poopay Ruella. Mrs Welles. What's her number? Quickly!

Harold 647.

Poopay 647 . . . 647. Can I borrow your key, please?

Harold My key? My pass key, you mean?

Poopay Just to get back in. Please, Harold. It's desperately important. Please.

Harold (*reluctantly handing key to her*) I want it straight back, you hear?

Poopay Thank you. I think she's in terrible danger . . .

Poopay goes out and the door closes behind her. Harold stares after her, indignantly.

Harold (*to the door*) So am I if someone catches me in here like this. (*He goes back into the bedroom.*)

The lights darken in the sitting room as we return to the other suite.
 Julian comes out of the bedroom, through the bathroom into the sitting room. He is manoeuvring a walking bundle. It is Ruella, her head and most of her body now covered in a thick hotel bedspread. Julian has secured this around her middle using the tie belt of her towelling robe. Indignant muffled shouts from Ruella as he manhandles her towards the window.

Julian Come on . . . that's it . . . this way . . .

They reach the windows. Julian opens them wide and guides Ruella out on to the balcony. As he does this, Poopay comes through the front door. She stops dead as she sees Julian.

Who the hell are you, then?

Poopay You take your hands off her, do you hear?

Julian stares at her.

Did you hear me? You touch her and I'll yell so loud you'll have everyone in this bloody hotel in here.

Julian (*unimpressed*) Why don't you just close that door?

Poopay What? I warn you, I'm going to yell.

Julian You even so much as open your mouth and she'll

be off this balcony faster than the speed of sound. Now close the door, please.

Poopay stands uncertain. Julian makes a sudden sharp movement, as if to push Ruella.

(*as he does this, sharply*) Close the door!

Poopay, startled, complies.

Now, come here. Come on. Come over here. I promise. I'll push her over if you don't.

Poopay You're going to push her anyway.

Julian (*playfully*) Who can tell? Come on . . .

Julian beckons her. Poopay moves cautiously towards him. As she passes the desk, in desperation she grabs up a paper knife and makes a lunge at Julian. He moves even faster. Pushing Ruella to the floor, he grasps Poopay's wrist and with ease, twists her into his arms, removing the knife as he does so. Poopay gasps.

(*starting to enjoy himself*) The only problem with using a weapon, is you have to make awfully sure that it doesn't get used on you instead. Do you see?

He appears to be about to use the knife on Poopay despite her efforts to wriggle out of his grip. At this moment, the communicating door swings open. Julian and Poopay become aware of this. Julian freezes, startled.
   The dark figure of a woman emerges. She begins to move slowly into the room. She is dressed entirely in black, including a hat. She is veiled.

Woman (*in a whisper*) Julian! . . . Julian! . . .

Poopay (*half under her breath*) Oh my God!

Julian stares at the woman in horror.

Woman (*holding out her arms to him, eerily*) Julian . . . It's me, Julian . . . remember me? Surely you remember me?

Julian, despite himself, takes a pace backwards, releasing Poopay.

Julian (*hoarsely*) Who are you? Who is it?

Woman It's me, Julian. You can't have forgotten your mother, Julian.

Julian Mother?

Woman Come back for you, at last . . . Come to me, Julian. Come to your mother. Look into my poor face. What did you do to my face, Julian?

The woman is very close to him. We see her better by the light from the window, but because of her veil, not yet her face.

Julian (*terrified*) No, Mother, no . . .

Woman Kiss me – JULIAN.

She throws back her veil to reveal the face of Death. Poopay screams.

(*hissing*) Joooooollllllian . . .

Julian (*covering his face with his arms and stepping backwards*) Motheeeeeeeerrrrrrr!

Julian has taken one pace too many. He loses his balance and falls backwards off the balcony.
The figure removes her hat and mask and leans over the parapet to see where he has landed. It is Jessica, now aged forty-five; a maturer, somewhat plumper version but largely unchanged.

Jessica (*looking down, pleased*) Golly . . . (*turning to Poopay*) You all right?

*Poopay nods. She is more in a state of shock from
Jessica's sudden appearance than from Julian's mauling.*

Hallo. I don't think we've met, have we? Jessica Rizzini.

Poopay Jessica – ?

Jessica I was Jessica Welles. About eleven years ago I was,
anyway. Reece's first wife, you know. Are you Phoebe by
any chance? You must be. Super.

*Poopay nods. Renewed noises from Ruella still tied up
under her bedspread and sitting on the floor of the
balcony. Jessica becomes aware of her.*

Sorry. Just a minute. Better let her out, poor thing.

The bundle makes more sounds.

(*shouting to Ruella*) It's all right. You're safe now, Ruella.
It's Jessica. Jessica. Just a second. I'm getting you out of
there.

*Jessica helps Ruella to her feet. She examines the
bathrobe belt around Ruella's waist.*

Hang on. Just find out how he's tied this. Oh I see, yes.
Simple enough. There you go.

*She pulls the belt off Ruella. Julian had tied it in a quick
release knot. The result is very nearly what Julian
planned to do. Ruella, still shrouded in the bedspread,
staggers back, sits on the edge of the balcony, teeters
back and forward, then topples off and disappears.*

Ruella (*as she goes*) Aaaaaaaaa!

Poopay No!

Jessica (*appalled*) Oh, help!

*Jessica and Poopay both manage to grab a piece of the
bedspread just before it disappears after Ruella.*

Poopay What did you do that for?

Jessica Sorry. She just sort of went. Oh, God! (*calling to the unseen Ruella*) Hold on! Hold on to this bedspread! Whatever you do, don't let go . . .

Ruella (*off, distant*) I have absolutely no intention of letting go . . .

Poopay Come on, let's try and . . . pull . . .

They both try to pull up the bedspread. It's too heavy for them. They give up.

Jessica This is hopeless. Oh, my nails . . .

Poopay (*breathless*) It's no good we can't get any – purchase on this – thing . . .

Ruella (*off*) Pull, for the love of God, pull!

Poopay (*calling*) We're trying.

Jessica (*agitatedly*) What are we going to do? What are we going to do?

Poopay Hang on. We need a sheet or something thinner. Can you hold her on your own, do you think? For a second?

Jessica (*alarmed*) On my own?

Poopay Just for a second? While I get a sheet.

Ruella (*off*) I am hanging several hundred feet up here. Just to remind you.

Poopay (*to Jessica*) Think you can hold her?

Ruella In case you'd both forgotten.

Jessica (*calling, rather irritably*) Yes we know, we know, we know. (*to Poopay*) All right I'll do my best.

Poopay Ready?

Jessica (*getting the best grip she can and bracing her feet*) Ready.

Poopay Right. I'm letting go – now.

Poopay does so. Jessica still clinging to the bedspread is virtually pulled straight over the balcony.

Ruella (*as she slips down further, off*) Aaaahh!

Jessica (*as she nearly goes over*) Aaaahhh!

Poopay manages to grab Jessica by the ankles.

Ruella (*off*) What the hell are you playing at, woman?

Jessica (*calling*) Sorry. I don't think I can hold this any longer.

Ruella Oh yes, you bloody well can.

Poopay (*to Jessica*) All right, don't try to move. Just hold on. I won't let go of you. I'm going to climb up you, to get a grip.

Jessica Up me? What do you mean up me?

Poopay Over you. Climb over you. Here I come.

Poopay starts to crawl hand over hand over Jessica who remains bent over the balcony.

Jessica (*to Poopay*) Ow! What are you doing? I feel like a pedigree Friesian.

Poopay I hate to think what that makes me. Just you keep hold of that bedspread. You let her go, I swear I'll push you straight after her.

Jessica I'm doing my best. Ow!

At last Poopay manages, while still keeping hold of Jessica, to grab on to the bedspread again.

Poopay Got it!

Jessica Well done! What do we do now?

Poopay I've no idea. Let me get my breath back.

Jessica At least you can breathe. This is agony.

Poopay It's not a lot of fun for her, is it? (*calling*) Ruella!

Ruella (*off*) I'm still here.

Poopay (*calling*) We're going to have another go at pulling you up, all right? Any help you can give us, we'd appreciate it –

Ruella (*off*) What do you want me to do? Come up there and help you?

Poopay (*calling*) No. I meant with your feet. If you can find any foot-holds once we start pulling.

Ruella (*off*) I'll do my best.

Jessica We'll never be able to pull her up. She's far too heavy.

Poopay We're going to have to, or else we'll die trying, all right? Are you ready?

Jessica (*muttering*) We'll never, never do it.

Poopay (*calling*) Ready, Ruella?

Ruella (*off*) Ready.

Poopay And – heave! And – heave! And – heave! Come on!

> *They start a series of tugs. The reverse of what they intend appears to be happening. Every time they tug, more and more of them goes over the balcony.*

Both (*continuing, gamely*) And – heave! And – heave! And – heave!

Ruella (*off*) I appear to be going down rather than up.

Poopay (*calling*) Yes, I know. So are we.

Jessica You're far too heavy. Why are you so *heavy*? (*tearfully*) What are we going to do?

Ruella (*off*) Well, for God's sake, don't cry. I've got enough problems without your nose running all over me.

Poopay (*with renewed determination*) Come on! And – heave! And – heave!

> *Harold chooses this moment to come through the front door. He gapes.*

Harold (*as he enters*) Now look, you left my key in this lock, didn't you – ?

Both (*unaware of him*) And – heave! And – heave!

Poopay (*to Jessica*) Come on! Come on! Put some effort into it!

Jessica I'm trying, I'm trying!

Poopay That's it, that's it. She's coming! She's coming!

Harold (*at the sight of this*) Oh, my God. (*He turns and flees the room again, closing the door.*)

> *At length, with several more 'And – heaves' Poopay and Jessica manage to haul Ruella over the balcony.*

Poopay
Jessica } (*together, triumphantly*) Yes!
Ruella

> *They all collapse in a heap on the balcony floor.*

Ruella (*breathless*) Close thing.

Jessica (*likewise*) Yes.

Poopay (*likewise*) Yes.

They sit, recovering their breath for a second.

Ruella I don't know about you two, but I think I'm in urgent need of the mini-bar.

Jessica Good idea.

Poopay Yes.

Ruella gets up and moves, a little uncertainly, to the sideboard. Poopay and Jessica follow suit.

Ruella Jessica, this is Phoebe. Remember I mentioned her?

Poopay Yes, we've met.

Ruella You gathered, Phoebe, that this is the first Mrs Welles. Jessica Welles.

Jessica Jessica Rizzini these days.

Ruella (*at the bar*) You've remarried?

Jessica Yes. In 1983. A couple of years after I left Reece.

Ruella Good for you. There's a small bottle of champagne here. Do we want that?

Jessica Perfect.

Poopay That'll do me.

Ruella starts to open the champagne and then pours three glasses during the next.

Ruella What's your husband do?

Jessica Rory? I'm not absolutely sure. But he's always terribly, terribly busy.

Ruella Ah. (*examining champagne*) God knows what this is like. Tell me, I must know – was it – was it my note that did it? Is that why you're here?

Jessica Let's say it sort of clinched things. I suppose if I hadn't got it, I might have stayed with Reece and . . . (*She tails away.*)

Poopay What was in this note, then?

Jessica Oh. Don't you know? Didn't she tell you? Just a second. It's inspired. (*She retrieves her bag and produces the note.*)

Ruella You haven't still got it?

Jessica Goes everywhere with me. (*holding up the envelope*) See? 'Not to be opened until 22 March 1975.'

Ruella You did as you were told, did you? You did wait?

Jessica With enormous self-control. For me.

Poopay And?

Jessica And. (*She unfolds the note carefully. It is quite faded and fragile now. Reading*) 'Congratulations. Yesterday you had your first child, a girl – 7lb 5oz . . .' 6oz, actually.

Ruella Sorry.

Jessica (*continuing to read*) '. . . 7lb 5oz. By now you have almost almost certainly named her Rachel Louise Elizabeth. Please God you will live to enjoy her.'

Poopay (*impressed*) Brilliant.

Ruella Thank you.

Poopay Proof positive.

Jessica Well, I think it was the PS about the caesarian that really convinced me, though.

Ruella hands out the glasses.

Thank you.

Poopay Ta.

Ruella Here's to . . . life, eh?

Poopay
Jessica } Life.

Ruella I'm awfully glad you did read that note. Quite apart from the fact that you're still here – it's also the reason I'm still here.

Jessica Oh, well. One good turn.

Ruella You did cut it a bit fine, if you don't mind my saying. I could have done with you a couple of seconds earlier. Lucky you came in when you did.

Jessica Well, it wasn't really that lucky. I spent all evening sitting in the dark in that store room next door.

Ruella Did you?

Jessica Spent a small fortune bribing the floor waiter. I sat there waiting to see if Julian turned up.

Ruella You might have told us.

Jessica Yes, I know it's awful but – even till just now I wasn't a hundred per cent sure. I mean, since you warned me against events that in the end never happened – thank God – because I avoided them, I had no real way of knowing if they ever would have happened anyway. If I hadn't avoided them. Do you see?

Ruella For God's sake, I predicted your baby.

Jessica It could have been a lucky guess.

Ruella Lucky guess!

Jessica Well, you know.

Ruella So you wanted to make sure he was actually going

to push me off that balcony before you decided to stop him?

Jessica No, I was always going to stop him. And I did. I thought I was rather good. I remember in the confession he'd said he killed his mother. I thought if I pretended to be her, I might give him a fright.

Ruella (*incredulously*) A fright?

Jessica I remember he was always showing me pictures of her. Terrifying-looking woman. Like a black widow spider.

Ruella (*still stunned*) Did you say fright? He had me trussed up in a bedspread about to shove me off the sixth floor and you thought you'd give him a *fright*? Don't you – forgive me – but don't you find that, as an overall game plan, just a fraction hit or miss?

Jessica I did have the gun, as well. Just in case.

Poopay Gun?

Jessica (*producing a small pistol from her bag*) This one. It's my husband, Rory's. I borrowed it. But I'm not an awfully good shot. I don't even know if it's loaded. (*She looks as if she might fire it.*)

Ruella (*ducking*) Put it away!

Jessica All right. (*She does.*) Rory's got masses of guns. He adores them. We have guns everywhere. He's promised to take me out soon, somewhere quiet, teach me to shoot.

Jessica has wandered to the window.

Ruella Really?

Poopay (*sotto, to Ruella*) I'm not coming back again to warn her. She's had her chance.

114

Ruella (*sotto, to Poopay*) She may just be one of those women that drive men to murder, poor thing.

Jessica (*looking over the balcony*) There's a huge crowd down there now.

Ruella Yes, well, don't start waving to them, dear, will you? We don't want them looking up here, do we?

Jessica Oh, no. (*She draws back.*) Sorry.

> *The door bell chimes. The three look apprehensive.*
> *Ruella goes to the door.*

Ruella (*calling*) Who is it?

Harold (*off*) Security. Harold Palmer.

Ruella (*to the others*) Oh, I'd forgotten about him . . .

> *Ruella opens the door to admit Harold. He enters rather cautiously.*

Harold Ah. All respectable now, are we?

Ruella I'm sorry?

Harold Listen, something very odd's just happened – (*seeing Jessica*) Ah. Good evening. Three of you now, is there?

Ruella Harold, you remember Jessica, Mr Welles' first wife . . .

Harold Oh, of course, yes . . . Very nice to see you again, Mrs – Mrs –

Jessica Rizzini. Countess Rizzini, actually.

Harold Countess. Yes. (*sotto*) Listen, there's been a – development . . .

Ruella Development?

Harold (*aware of Jessica*) The property with which we were dealing, that which was defunct has – re-animated.

Poopay Eh?

Harold The – deceased object with which we were dealing –

Ruella It's all right, Harold, we can talk in front of Jessica – the countess.

Harold Oh, right. Well, he's gone. I was strewing a few garments around the bedroom, I turn round, his body's vanished off the bed.

Poopay Vanished?

Ruella How interesting. Yes, it would. Of course it would.

Harold So he can't have been dead, can he? (*to Poopay*) You were right. I could have sworn he was dead. He must have just got up off the bed and walked out when my back was turned. Probably still concussed.

Ruella Could be.

Harold This is not going to look good, is it? A naked man in a coma wandering around the place. I need to find him before he gets to the public areas. (*His bleeper goes off.*) Excuse me. My pager. (*He takes it from his pocket and examines it.*) 'Incident in street.' What the hell does that mean?

Ruella Oh dear.

Harold This is one of those nights. Just one of those nights. Excuse me. (*He goes out, closing the door.*)

Jessica What was all that about?

Ruella It's – I think it's simply a case that you can't be in two places at once. Or even dead twice. It really isn't important now. It's all past history.

Jessica (*finishing her champagne*) Well, thank you for that. Bedtime for me, I think. Get a couple of hours, anyway . . . We're back to Rome in the morning. (*to Ruella*) Ruella, we must meet up. Have lunch together or something. Next time we're in London.

Ruella That would be lovely. Once I've divorced Reece, I'm as free as a bird.

Jessica You are going to divorce him, then?

Ruella Wouldn't you?

Jessica I did.

Ruella Yes, of course.

Jessica Perhaps without Julian, he might be a lot nicer. Now. I mean Julian was a terribly bad influence on Reece, wasn't he?

Ruella Dreadful.

Jessica (*to Poopay*) Goodnight, nice to have met you. Perhaps you'd like to have lunch as well.

Poopay Actually, I'm a bit young. I'm only technically about thirteen at the moment.

Jessica Thirt – ? Oh, I see. Yes. Well, no, I don't see. Not at all. It's far too complicated for me.

Jessica opens the door.

Ruella By the way, how's Rachel? Is she still in the States?

Jessica The States?

Ruella At university?

Jessica No, she's at Cambridge. Surely you knew?

Ruella No, I didn't. Things have obviously – changed. Cambridge? That's nice.

Jessica Don't think she's ever been to the States, actually. Very brainy. Quite alarmingly so. Don't know where she gets it from. 'Night.

Ruella Goodnight.

Poopay 'Night.

Jessica leaves, closing the door.
A silence. Poopay is very subdued.

Ruella You're very quiet. All right?

Poopay Yes, I was just . . . You know. Working up the energy to go home.

Ruella Do you want to? Go back, I mean?

Poopay I can't stay here, can I?

Ruella No, I don't think you could. I have a feeling that – if you stayed here you might – well, God knows what would happen if you ever met your younger self, for instance.

Poopay What, me at thirteen? I wouldn't fancy meeting that.

Ruella Where's your home? Where did you used to live? In these days?

Poopay Streatham.

Ruella Oh. Not far. What were – what are your parents? What do they do for a living?

Poopay I don't know. I never knew.

Ruella No?

Poopay It was a children's home.

Ruella Oh, I see. I'm sorry.

An awkward pause. This is not something Poopay likes to talk about.

Well, I'll go and visit you, if you like . . .

Poopay No. . . .

Ruella Take you out to tea.

Poopay Don't bother. Please. I tell you, I was horrible at that age. Real delinquent. If you're going to remember me, remember me like this, all right? (*holding out her hand, rather awkwardly*) Thank you. Very much.

Ruella What for? Thank *you*.

Poopay It's been really good to know you. I think you're somebody really quite . . . I'll go now or I'll cry. I always cry when I say goodbye to people. Pathetic. Dominatrix. Always in floods of tears.

Ruella You're going back to that?

Poopay Probably, yes.

Ruella Why not? Do you do well? I mean, do you make lots of money?

Poopay It's not what it was. I'm too old-fashioned, really. Only get the older clientèle. It's all this technology nowadays. VS.

Ruella VS?

Poopay Virtual sex. They're all sitting at home. Mouse in one hand, joystick in the other.

Ruella Not much fun that, surely?

Poopay No effort, though. Don't have to bother. Never have to move. You get bored you switch it off.

Ruella Have a go at something else.

Poopay Me? Like what, for instance? It's a very competitive world up that way. No free goes, no second rides. Warn your kids. If you're not qualified, you die. Don't let them do what I did . . . (*She moves towards the communicating door.*) Tell you what – I've got a great idea – what date is it now where I am – ? yes, all right. Listen, on July 26th 2014 – that's tomorrow, my time – come to this hotel, nine o'clock at night, if you can make it and we'll have a drink downstairs. There's a nice bar by then called Judi's. Is it a date?

Ruella Phoebe, I'll be ancient by then . . .

Poopay Date?

Ruella I'll be sixty – whatever. (*relenting*) OK. It's a date. If I'm around.

Poopay opens the door.

Poopay You make sure you are. Good luck with your divorce. If you have one.

Ruella Unless I can find one single good reason to stick with the man.

Poopay (*laughing*) You never know. He may improve. They sometimes do, you know. Just when you think it's hopeless. Bye.

Poopay closes the door. Ruella stands for a second, thoughtfully. She is working on an idea. She smiles to herself.

Ruella (*to herself*) Hmm! Maybe. (*She moves towards the bedroom.*) Maybe! (*She switches off the lights and goes into the bedroom.*)

In the lobby, Poopay revolves. She steps out into the darkened room. Just a light from the bedroom. She creeps across the room and falls over the same object of furniture as before.

Poopay (*disgusted with herself*) Oh!

Reece (*from the bedroom*) Who's that? Who's that out there?

> *Poopay freezes. Reece comes out of the bedroom and turns on the lights. He is seventy years old again but in much better physical shape than previously. His manner is altogether more positive. He carries a photo album.*

(*seeing her*) Who the – ? Phoebe! Hallo, darling, what are you doing here, creeping about in the dark?

Poopay (*confused*) I –

Reece Lovely to see you – why didn't you tell me you were coming? What a nice surprise. What brings you to town?

> *Poopay's voice, her accent, her whole delivery has changed, as much to her own amazement as anyone's.*

Poopay I was just passing. I'm awfully sorry if I woke you up . . . (*she looks puzzled. Repeating*) . . . woke you up. (*She feels her throat and tastes her tongue.*)

Reece Oh, you know me, I wasn't asleep. Sit down, sit down for a minute. Go on.

Poopay Well, literally for a second. (*She repeats the business.*)

Reece You all right?

Poopay Yes.

Reece Got a sore throat?

Poopay No.

Reece I've got some Fisherman's Friends in there. Found a shop in Hammersmith that still sells them, would you believe?

Poopay Really? How wonderful . . . (*She smacks her lips again.*)

Reece Want a drink, then?

Poopay No, I'm fine. I promise.

Reece (*sitting next to her*) Couldn't sleep at all. Never can these days. (*Pause. Sadly*) It'll be a year next month, you know. Since she went. Still miss her dreadfully, Phoebe. Always will, I suppose. Bound to.

Poopay (*suddenly aware to whom he's referring*) Oh.

Reece Don't you?

Poopay Oh, yes. Yes.

Reece I think we two were closest to her, you know. Well – apart from Thomas, I suppose. But you can never really tell with Tom, can you? Rue and I would have been married thirty-two years last June. And do you know, in all that time, never once did we . . . never.

Poopay (*smiling*) What, never? Come on . . .

Reece Well. We had our moments, I suppose. Nothing serious. Usual thing. I got busy, she got broody. I said to her for God's sake we've got two of them, woman, what do you want more for? We've made our point. She said, I want another. You're too busy and I'm too old, so I'm adopting. I said to her, well, for God's sake get a kid with character. And she did. (*smiling*) Quite a decent one, too, by the time she'd finished with you. (*Pause.*) Bloody awful illness. They find a cure for one thing, along comes another. Nature's sick joke. At least this one was quick.

Poopay I'm sorry.

Reece Amazing woman, you know. Kept me on the rails. Sorted us all out in our time, didn't she?

Poopay (*smiling*) Yes . . .

Reece (*showing her the book*) Look at this, what I dug out just now. (*a loose photo*) Look at you two there. That was in Antigua. Two brown beauties. More like sisters.

Poopay Yes. And there with Rachel.

Reece With Rachel. That's when Rue was expecting Tom. There's me, would you believe? (*another photo*) Ah, there's poor old Julian. You remember Julian, or was he before your time? I forget.

Poopay I – heard about him.

Reece Tragic. Must have been drunk. Only explanation. I owed him a lot, too, you know.

Poopay Yes. (*she rises*) Dad, I ought to go. I'm sorry. You need some sleep.

Reece (*rising*) Yes, I'll try and get an hour or so. (*giving her the album*) Here, take this with you. I just found it. It was in among all those packing cases next door. (*He moves to the window.*) Take it home. Show it to Robert and the kids.

Poopay (*as if remembering them*) Robert and the kids. Oh, yes . . . (*She smiles.*)

Reece Give them a laugh. (*He stands, looking out.*)

Poopay (*moving to him*) Quiet out there tonight. Is this truce going to last?

Reece It might this time. We live in hope. Lewisham have agreed to sign. It's only Croydon being difficult as usual . . . At least everyone's still talking. That's the important thing. We're having another go at them tomorrow.

Poopay Then try and sleep. We're all relying on you.

Reece Me? I'm just there to bang their heads together, that's all. (*He moves towards the bedroom door.*) You brought your car, I hope?

Poopay Oh, yes.

Reece Well, take care on your way home. Nowhere's safe these days, I tell you. Not even this place, knee deep in security guards . . .

Poopay It's all right, Dad, I can take care of myself. Don't worry . . .

Reece When I was young, you know, when I came to this hotel for my first honeymoon, there was just one man – mark you, one single man – who was responsible for the entire security of this building. And we never had a jot of trouble. Not a jot. Can you believe that?

Poopay What happened to him?

Reece Who?

Poopay The one security man?

Reece No idea. Dead by now, I should imagine. No, hang on. I do remember. Harold – Parker? Palmer. That's it. Harold Palmer. That's right. He inherited some money, from an old aunt or something. Jacked it all in and bought himself a boat. Knowing Harold, it probably sank off Malta with all hands. Switch off when you leave, will you?

Poopay Dad, are you all right here? On your own? Stuck in this hotel, I mean?

Reece Oh, yes . . .

Poopay You're not getting lonely? I mean, we'd always be happy to –

Reece No, no, it suits me fine at the moment. It's convenient for the job. I'll come and visit you, I promise.

That's the way to do it. Short visits, then you miss me. I see a lot of Rachael these days, you know. She's working not far away. And I even see Tom. Sometimes.

Poopay Well, remember . . . that's all.

Reece kisses her.

Reece You come and see me again soon, Phoebe, when you can. You're very special to me, you know.

Poopay I will.

Reece If you can ever tear yourself away from your drawing board . . .

Poopay Computer, Dad, computer. I promise.

Reece Only next time, make it the daytime, not the middle of the night, there's a love. 'Night.

Poopay 'Night.

Reece goes into the bedroom and closes the door. Poopay walks to the front door slowly. She pauses at the doorway and opens the photo album. She picks out the loose photo of her and Ruella, looks at it for a second or so, smiles, replaces it and then closes the book.

(*softly, still smiling*) Thank you. (*She turns off the sitting room lights and goes.*)

BLACKOUT